Young**Writers** 2005 PO

PLAYGROUND

Let your creativity flow...

Southern England Vol II
Edited by Heather Killingray

 Young**Writers**

First published in Great Britain in 2005 by:
Young Writers
Remus House
Coltsfoot Drive
Peterborough
PE2 9JX
Telephone: 01733 890066
Website: www.youngwriters.co.uk

SB ISBN 1 84602 214 2

Foreword

Young Writers was established in 1991 and has been passionately devoted to the promotion of reading and writing in children and young adults ever since. The quest continues today. Young Writers remains as committed to the fostering of burgeoning poetic and literary talent as ever.

This year's Young Writers competition has proven as vibrant and dynamic as ever and we are delighted to present a showcase of the best poetry from across the UK. Each poem has been carefully selected from a wealth of *Playground Poets* entries before ultimately being published in this, our thirteenth primary school poetry series.

Once again, we have been supremely impressed by the overall high quality of the entries we have received. The imagination, energy and creativity which has gone into each young writer's entry made choosing the best poems a challenging and often difficult but ultimately hugely rewarding task - the general high standard of the work submitted amply vindicating this opportunity to bring their poetry to a larger appreciative audience.

We sincerely hope you are pleased with our final selection and that you will enjoy *Playground Poets Southern England Vol II* for many years to come.

Contents

Anais King (10)	28
Sophie Utting (11)	28
Trixie Roddick (10)	29
Anton Capstack (11)	29
Alex Hall (9)	30
Alex Morgan (11)	30
Jade Savage (11)	31
Marko Stojanovic (11)	31
Sophie Eager (11)	32
Ema Stojanovic (11)	32
Dheeraj Ahluwalia (9)	33
Evan Richardson (11)	33
Imogen Hay (11)	34
Daleep Singh (10)	34
Charlie Corcoran (10)	35
Aran McGroarty (11)	35
Emily Bonsor (10)	36
Joshua Weekly (11)	36
Charlotte Smith (9)	37
William Barnard (10)	37
Daniel Hallstrom (10)	38
Jemma Guile (11)	38
Stephanie Babb (10)	39
Ellie Roberts (9)	39
Lucy Lowe (9)	40
Eva Steinhardt (10)	40
Octavia Pearce (10)	41
Beatrice Clegg (10)	41
Alex Dilley (9)	42
Stephanie Wright (10)	43
Lily Thomas (10)	44
Anna McMurtrie (10)	45

Inkpen Primary School, Hungerford

Alex Childs (9)	46
Kerry Faulkner (9)	46
Lloyd Childs (11)	46
Lucy Dodridge (11)	47
Conor Hurst (10)	47
Max Butterworth (9)	47
Amy Hooper (11)	48

Hannah Warrick (11)   48
Jack Henry Bailey-Bale (10)   49
Alix Wiltshire (10)   49
Holly Titford (11)   50
Kimberley Johnson (9)   51
Adrian Wells (11)   51

Kempshott Junior School, Basingstoke
Richard Butler (11)   52
Will Smith (11)   52
Ashley Brown (11)   53
Stuart Locke (10)   53
Hannah Ulysses (11)   54
Thomas Quayle (11)   55
Rhiann Sallows (11)   56
Lauren James (11)   57
Zoe Comerford (11)   58
Amy Steel (11)   59
Hayley Moore (11)   60
Chloe Udal (10)   60
Olivia White (11)   61
Scott Coomber (11)   61
Guy Pope (11)   62
Mark Nickell (10)   63
Sophie Webb (11)   64
Elliot Bateman (11)   64
Becky Curtis-Harris (11)   65
Kelly Cummings (11)   65
Laura Smith (11)   66
John Venner (11)   67
Evienne Heynes (10)   68
Jazmine Johnson (11)   68
Rhianne Rampton (11)   69
Alistair Miller (11)   70
Pooja Rabheru (11)   71
Terry Sibley (10)   72
Toby Foley (11)   73
Amber Connolly (11)   74
Sian Swyny (11)   75
Gabriella Clarke (11)   76
Richard Oliver (11)   76

Sam Nightingale (11)	77
Andrew Allen (11)	77
Ryan Case (11)	78
Andrew Spencer (11)	78
Jamie Kelly (11)	79
Camilla Johnson (11)	79
Hannah Owens (11)	80
Georgina Smith (11)	80
Chris Smith (11)	81
Jack Hallinan (11)	81
Kimberley Parrott (11)	82
Deanna Moss (11)	82

Kingswood Primary School, Tadworth

Ellie Cameron (9)	83
Greg Fowler (10)	83
Michael Newman (10)	84
Tony Graham (10)	84
Danni Gibbs (9)	84
Catriona Barber (10)	85
Gemma East (10)	85
Jodie Fahey (10)	86
Charlene Lok (9)	86
Oliver Hazel (10)	87
Harry Naef (10)	87
Lauren Simmons (10)	88
Stephanie Clarke (10)	88
Ella Beagley (10)	88
Sian Wells (9)	89

Lytchett Matravers Primary School, Poole

Adrian Hobbs (8)	89
Samantha Hacklett (8)	90
Shannon Johnson (8)	90
Chelsea Carter (8)	91
Nathaniel Long (8)	91
Eleanor Walls (7)	92
Erin Hopper (7)	92
Amy Barr (8)	93
Hollie Bryant (8)	93
Lucy Farrant (8)	94

Ben Sharman (9)	94
Lucas Jones (8)	95
Sidney Longworth (9)	95
Ben Short (7)	95
Dhiren Leal (9)	96
Charlie Dennett (8)	96
George Wood (9)	97
James Belchamber (8)	97
Callum Whiteford (7)	98
Sarah Ayley (9)	98
Holly Miles (8)	99
Lauren Graham (8)	99
Annabel Mulholland (9)	100
Becky Downs (9)	100
Matt Holland (9)	101
Xander Ettling (9)	101
Charlotte Miles (9)	102
Daniel Lake (8)	102
Megan Single (8)	102
Charlotte Rubenstein (9)	103
George Woods (9)	103
Christopher Pillinger (9)	103
Jodie Ellis (8)	104
Megan Ackrell (8)	104
Patricia Baldwin (9)	105
Libby Lamb (8)	105
William Fowler (9)	106
Emily Chamberlain (9)	106
Lauren Lloyd-Evans (8)	106
Megan Horlock (9)	107
Jade Rumens (8)	107
James Duncan (8)	108
Natalie Taylor (9)	108
Lauren Churchill (9)	109
Luca Infante (9)	109
Daniel Amey (9)	110
Naleisha Fisk (9)	110
Jessica Taylor (8)	110
Gemma Cane (9)	111
Lara Pattison (8)	111
Sam de Garis (8)	111
Lauren Collins (9)	112

Lewis Blair (9)	112
Scott Horlock (9)	112
Millie Morgan (8)	113
Oliver Matthews (9)	113
Oliver Levy (9)	114
Rebecca Lewis (9)	114
Mitchell Taylor (9)	115
Gavin Brown (8)	115
Mark Scoble (7)	115
Jack Hawkins (9)	116
Ben de Garis (8)	116
Hannah Barr (10)	117
Ryan Churchward (8)	117
Jessica Lake (10)	118
Georgia Collins (8)	118
Jenny Matthews (10)	119
Charli Webster (8)	119
Rosemary Walls (10)	120
Tommy Holden (9)	121
Maelle Swann (10)	122
Rory Hover (8)	122
Caitlin McCarthy (9)	123
Eliza Atkinson (8)	123
Richard Tolson (10)	124
Hannah Maese (9)	124
Rebecca Tummon (8)	124
Charlotte Ettling (10)	125
Mollie Heap (8)	125
Louis Castle (10)	126
Georgina Hart (9)	126
Sam Scriven (10)	127
Andrew Hillman (8)	127
Taylor Broom (9)	128
Michael Prince (10)	128
Ellen Taylor (10)	129
Matt Burton (10)	129
Hollymay Gladwin (10)	130
Abbey Butterworth (9)	131
Stefan Webster (10)	132
Toby Wonnacott (10)	132
Katie Dechow (10)	133
Lacy Dominey (8)	133

Emily Atkinson (10)	134
Andrew Sofianos (10)	134
Gemma Hart (10)	135
Jodie Peters (10)	135
Katie Gillion (10)	136
Louisa Styles (10)	136
Megan Alexander (9)	137

Meeching Valley Primary School, Newhaven

Jack Hammond (10)	137
Liam Dolan (11)	137
Alice Fuller (10)	138
Katrina Matthews (11)	138
Richard Taylor (11)	138
Laura Coley (11)	139
Natasha Parton (11)	139
Oliver Barron-Carter (11)	139
Emily Cornford (11)	140
Hannah Deakin (10)	140
Josh Sarrou (11)	140
Rebecca Kite (11)	141
Sebastian Saunders (11)	141
Emma Rix (11)	141
Kadie Wright (11)	142

Park Hill Junior School, Croydon

Chevron Phillips-McLean (9)	142
Callum Mance (8)	143
Matthias Comrie (8)	143
Shuoh-Fuu Tang (9)	144
Aliya Ismailova (8)	145
Aman Berry (9)	146
Declan Card (9)	146
Elizabeth Hillier (9)	147
Luke Adams (9)	147
Gil Yehezkel (9)	148
Stephanie Eid (9)	148
Victor Mendon (9)	149
Amal Nadeem (8)	149
Nikhil Patel (8)	150
Ryan Doherty (9)	151

Pickhurst Junior School, West Wickham

Joe Morilla (9)	182
Victoria Munt (10)	183
Siân Semerey (9)	183
Jazmine Wilkinson (10)	184
Oliver Saunders (10)	184
Alexzandra Vlahovic (10)	185
Joe Darbourne (11)	185
Geneviève Zane (11)	186
Emily Briant (9)	187
Ben Card (8)	187
Faith Hawthorn (8)	188
Hannah Penning (7)	188
Eden Ansell (8)	189
Maria Martin (7)	189
Lottie Ballard (10)	190
Sarah Baldon (8)	190
James Lanckmans (10)	191
Lily Outram (8)	191
Daniel Carpenter (10)	192
Emma Sullivan (8)	192
Ellen Simmons (10)	193
Victoria Smith (10)	194
Phoebe Blunt (10)	194
Amy Jardine (10)	195

St Michael's Junior School, Aldershot

Sean Sussex (9)	195
Leah Paget (9)	196
Daisy West (9)	197
Micheal Hayes (10)	198
Daniel Sullivan (9)	198
Paige Powell (10)	199
Hannah Cole (9)	199
Layla Swindell (9)	200
Rebecca Neve (10)	201
Connor A Tomlinson (9)	202
Tristan Tatarek (9)	202
Kimberley Homer (10)	203
Bryony Reed (9)	203
Josh Ward (9)	204
Megan Paynton (10)	205

St Peter's Catholic Primary School, Shoreham-by-Sea

Camilla Haywood (11)	205
Joseph Sivver (11)	206
Elysia Fawn (11)	206
Natalie Dalpadado (11)	207
Ryan Bethune (11)	207
Joe McLoughlin (11)	208
Jack Fry (11)	208
Toby Kelly (11)	209
James Topliff (11)	209
Joshua Jewiss (11)	210
Aisling Butler (11)	210
Charlotte Anderson (11)	211
Colin Colas (11)	211
Callum Farrell (11)	212
Gemma Coyle (10)	212
Rhys Garrish (10)	212
Anne Ballard (11)	213
Robyn James (11)	213
Sam Russell (11)	214
Katie Hart (11)	214
Nageswaran Kalidasan (11)	215

Singlewell CP School, Gravesend

Rachael Smith (10)	216
Billy Luker (8)	216
Anne-Marie Wilson (7)	217
Sam Goddard (7)	217
Heidi Gaskin (8)	218
Francesca Bonfield (8)	218
Amber Hollins (8)	218
Claire Morris (7)	219
Megan Ayley (7)	219
Jessica Hunt (8)	220
Nicola Thompson (7)	220
Chantay White (8)	221
Charlotte Brown (7)	221
Hannah Cox (8)	221
Jamie Gilbert (8)	222
Chloe Kitchen (7)	222

Callum Cherrison (8)	222
Bethany Chuter (9)	223
Megan Salter (9)	223
Holly Hewitt (9)	224
Kelly Gardiner (8)	224
Heather Robertson (9)	225
Rebecca Johnson (8)	225
Luke Thompson (9)	226
Callum Howes (8)	226
Patrick Mitchell (9)	227
Lewis Wade (9)	227
Jack Wade (9)	228
James Bell (9)	228
Rachael Cox (10)	229
Jessica Hutton (10)	229
Natalie Hickmott (11)	230
Charley Whyte (9)	230
Josh Law (11)	231
Amy Rolfe (9)	231
Alice Ellison (10)	232
Sarah Lane (10)	232
Hollie Mason (11)	233
Rachael Hurcombe (10)	233
Tony Lambert (10)	234
Elisha Waghorn (10)	234
Emily Liquorish (11)	235
Ria Gwalter (10)	235
Rory Newman (11)	236
Ian Thompson (10)	236
Anna Rolfe (10)	236
Jack Baldwin (10)	237
James Flaherty (10)	237
Lucy Hickmott (10)	237
Bethany Sibun (11)	238
Ben May (10)	238
Hannah Toulson (9)	239
Hayley Rolf (10)	239
Jodie Gibbs (10)	240
Andrew Windsor (10)	240
Daniella Bates (11)	240
Mitchell Dossetter (10)	241

Shannon Bailey (9)	261
Charlotte King (10)	261
Lisa Dutton (9)	262
Kayley Emmett (9)	263
Jordan Alder (9)	264
Yasmin Ali (8)	265
Chelsea Cowley (9)	266
Toni Kelsey (9)	267
Martin Hunt (9)	268
Omar Beaumont (10)	268
Andrew Mwaki (10)	269
Jinny Chonde (9)	270
David Annetts (9)	271
Karina Beckford (8)	272
Jonathan Ivell & Courtney Saunders (9)	273
Rachel Chonde (11)	274
Georgia Cannon (9)	275
Terri Trimby (11)	276
Vanessa Asongo (11)	276
Joseph Brawn (11)	277
Lannetha Williams (11)	277
Richie Locke (11)	278
Tony Trimby (11)	278
Tiah-Louise Flynn (10)	279

Woodmansterne Primary School, Banstead

Lucie Ellison (8)	279
Claire Palmer (9)	280
Harry Teal (9)	280
Caolan Quinn (9)	281
Joseph Emanuel (8)	281
Charlotte Stokoe (9)	282
Brooke Jones (9)	282
Lauren Jennings (9)	283
Megan Grover (9)	283
Joshua Noon (8)	283
Harry Cartwright (8)	284
Thomas McFarlane (9)	284
Liam Turner (8)	284
Georgia Thomas (10)	285

The Poems

The Collector

I am 'The Collector'
I collect
Strange beasts.
In my collection
There is:
The 'Aqua-Lion'
The 'Living Cheese'
The 'Scale Bird'
Among many, many others,
But!
To complete it
I need
The flying snake!

There
In the field I was
Waiting, hoping, fearing
All I wanted was a glimpse
And then . . .

It was so tiny, so thin
I almost missed it
I could have got it
But it was too quick
It whirled around my head
Teasing me
I almost had it
It slipped out of my fingers
Out of my reach
And then
The flying snake
Was gone.

Polly Sandiford-Ward (10)
Carlton Hill Primary School, Brighton

Walking To The Lanes

As we turn the corner
I saw a zebra on the house.
After that I saw some bikes chained up outside the bike shop.
The show made a shadow.

When I saw the beautiful colourful sweets
I loved the smell of those sweets.
After that shop I saw a hairdresser.
It was a beautiful sunny day.
The sweets' flavours are banana and strawberry.

I could smell sweets, chocolate and cooking.
I can hear music, babies crying, people talking and people walking.
I can see people, sweets, chocolates and cookies.

Then my grandad gave me £1.50.
I was sunbathing on the grass.
Animals were eating,
Butterflies flying on the grass.

Josh Berry (10)
Carlton Hill Primary School, Brighton

The Lanes

Just around the corner in The Lanes,
Cafés and shops were just opening,
A heavenly smell drifted out of the open bakery door.

Peer through the wide see-through glass,
We clenched our fists in excitement,
A couple of clouds in the clear blue sky.

The lunch boxes were protected by the glass,
Waiting to be looked at,
The smell of cookies blew my way.

People and music were heard,
I was the only one that noticed a plane and
A dead bird.
I saw a butterfly and a blackbird soaring around.

Maria Mellis (10)
Carlton Hill Primary School, Brighton

Jade Doesn't Like Answering Questions

Jade doesn't like answering questions,
It's not that she hasn't got any ideas,
It's that she thinks it's the wrong answer.

When the teacher asks her,
She starts to get worried.

Everyone laughs . . . except Jade.
Everyone laughs . . . except Jade.

The teacher thinks it's OK,
She has to try,
She can't always rely on others.

Jade doesn't understand,
That her teacher is making it fair,
And because of that,
Jade thinks she is being put on the spot.

Kodi Howell (11)
Carlton Hill Primary School, Brighton

Walking Through The Lanes

As I turned the corner,
There was a building dressed as a zebra.
Shadows strolled beside people.

The mouth watering gobstopper dragged me into Caramella.
The bicycle wheel shone like a sparkling star.

Through the glass, a Darth Vader mask,
Shiny and black reflecting the sun.
I stopped at Shake Away,
150 shakes, strawberry, Yorkie and Flake
were my favourite.

I smelt the gorgeous cookies from Ben's Cookies.
My favourite is coconut.
After I went to the Pavilion Gardens,
Birds were singing, butterflies were flying like angels.

Michael Serrao (11)
Carlton Hill Primary School, Brighton

The Playground

Outside I rush,
To play.
On a blazing
Hot summer's day.

Round the playground
I dash,
Hear children fiddle
With games they have
Brought in from home.

Turn round the bend,
I'm at the woodchips,
The dust stings my eyes,
It blows in the breeze,
Hear the chains rattle.

On the football pitch,
See people moan,
Unfair teams, goals
Disallowed.
Whistle blown
Break over.

Luke Wade (11)
Carlton Hill Primary School, Brighton

A Stroll In The Lanes

I enter the lanes,
        A cool light breeze brushes my hair
Forfars bakery,
          Pulling
              Me in with its sweet aroma.
Seagulls swooping in front of Forfars' door.

On I walk
Stop at a sweet shop
Pick the
Sweets and
Gobble them all up
With my sugar-coated hands.

On I walk
A Darth Vader cut-out
          Glares out of his mask and into my eyes
Oils and incense swirling round my nose
          Making me dizzy.

Up I look,
A sea of clouds hangs in the sky like time has stopped.
I rest,
And lick my ice lolly.
Out of a bush a small brown bird hops
To steal my ice lolly, it succeeds.

Cleary Mallard (11)
Carlton Hill Primary School, Brighton

Walking Through The Lanes

Seven bikes chained to the post,
Sunlight reflecting bicycle wheels and windowpanes,
A house painted like a zebra.

Sweet shops grab me and pulled me into the Caramella to buy
Different types of sugar.
Blueberry sweets stain my thieving hands.

Down around the corner,
We plod,
Red ribbons grab my attention, dancing all over to the sky.
Thirty jewels flash to my eyes like a shining sun.
A fast car running to The Lanes like a man mounting a
                                        Speedy horse.

Pigeons flying all over to the Pavilion Gardens to see if
There's any food to eat.
Seagulls walking to the shadows to cool themselves -
I ate ice-cold lollies.

Ronmar Trajano (10)
Carlton Hill Primary School, Brighton

The Lanes!

As I peered round the corner,
The smell of bread took over my senses.
A crowd of zebras left their stripes behind,
Leaving the building black, white and bold.

The sun gazed over my shoulder,
The rings in the jewellery shop glittered
Like a slug in the sky, a plane left a train behind.

Stopping for a break,
I saw all of the shopkeepers putting chairs out,
And the smell of sweets with the whistling of music,
Travelling along with the breeze.

The shops full of bags,
The smell of ice cream,
And the day completed with a song.

As I walked into the Pavilion Gardens
The grass covered my legs.
Meanwhile the seagulls were waiting to eat our rubbish.

Madeeha Chowdhury (11)
Carlton Hill Primary School, Brighton

The Lanes

Clouds drift my thoughts,
Just around the corner a
Zebra house leapt into view.

On the road to the shops
Loud music going through me.
Sweet shops reminded me of Saturdays.

Red ribbons hung like a necklace
Around my neck.

The fresh air smelt like candyfloss.

All around I could hear
People chatting
Drills drilling,
Shops opening and buggies were
Moving sounding like trains.

Footsteps were clapping
Cars were running
And music was beating like a heart.

Wandering home birds were fighting
Over scraps it made me think of food.

Paige Redman (11)
Carlton Hill Primary School, Brighton

The Lanes

Round the bend
The Lanes glide into view.
Market stools flanking the streets.

On the busy Lanes road
We look stunned,
Then stop.
We enter the shop
Without thinking,
We nick cherry jelly-beans
Pink rose juice
Stains our greedy tongues.

Through the street we walk
Stop at a nightclub.
We can see a café,
Hear music like a heartbeat,
And smell the aromatic sensation of iced brownies.

We stop to take a look at wildlife,
Seagulls are gliding,
Pigeons scrambling over scraps,
We relax over ice cream.

Imaya Bowen-Long (10)
Carlton Hill Primary School, Brighton

The Lanes

Round the corner I turned,
Shops leapt into range.
The sun,
A laser in my eyes.
A zebra print splashed across an eye-catching house.

As I passed the sleepy shops,
A slow beat filled the street.
Mouth watering chocolate smells danced in the wind,
Sugar stuck to our hungry hands.

Fiery red ribbons up high,
Sway gently.
The wonderful smell of leather,
Came from pink, white, black and blue shoes.
The noise of buggies rattling on the pavement.

The dog bounded over the arched fence.
The narrow crane glimmered in the sunlight.
Chimes rang in my ears,
A quick glance at my watch.
Time to go.

Jasmin Blake (11)
Carlton Hill Primary School, Brighton

The Lanes

The breeze brushed my face
I dawdled around the corner,
Clear blue sky above
Bikes reflecting light.

A grand sweet shop
Magnificent amount of sweets,
Scrumptious ice cream
Stained our piggish mouths,
I breathed in the mouth watering
Aroma of the chocolate chip cookies.

All that was around me
Was abandoned ashtrays.
There was a slight sound
Of music from a far distance away.

We sunbathed at the magnificent Pavilion
And had some scrumptious ice cream.
As we were sunbathing
We caught sight of lots of insects in the grass,
The beautiful birds flying in the daytime breeze.

Pavandeep Singh (11)
Carlton Hill Primary School, Brighton

The Lanes

Just around the corner of The Lanes
I saw a building
With stripes like a zebra
Spring into view.
Dummies watch
As people in T-shirts stroll past.

We stopped at Caramella,
Our greedy hands filled with sticky sweets.
The smell reminded me of Sundays
Where I get sweets.
I went to my mum's shop,
But she wasn't there.

James Bond reaches for chocolate, stacked high.
Sunlight catches jewellery and sequinned bags
Glittery and bright.

We sat down at the Pavilion Gardens
The grass, green, soft and cool.
Ice cream, cold, sweet and yummy.

Enrico Kin LeMaistra (10)
Carlton Hill Primary School, Brighton

The Lanes

Turned corner,
Saw a spinning sign.
Spinning flower looking at the sea of sky
No icebergs in the blue.

Walk forward for a minute
See a sweet shop,
Slip in,
See sherbet saucers,
Snatch them quick
Carefully! Carefully!
Out without detection
Munch! Crunch! Yum!

Glimpse millions of shops,
Not many customers.
Smell piece of chocolaty Heaven
Hear thumping of my guilty heart.

Look around and see
Birds moored to the ground by
Invisible anchors.

Jacob Bennett-Woolf (11)
Carlton Hill Primary School, Brighton

The Lanes

Peering round the corner,
A zebra's stripes were left behind.
Refreshing breezes stole the sun's warmth.

I pass 'Resident'
Full to the brim with music,
It's Heaven to my ears.
I smell the food across the road.

Guitars: Treasure enclosed behind golden bars!
The key is held
By one guitar god alone!

As I stop for the last time,
Not for any stool or shop,
But a park! I sit and lick ice cold lollies.

My time in the lanes,
Unlike my money,
Was well spent.

Smigl Greenland (11)
Carlton Hill Primary School, Brighton

Sunny Skies Over The Lanes

Sauntering round a small street bend,
A bakery mixes my imagination.
The heat of the sun keeping me sweating.

On the concrete path we plod,
And notice ribbons above
Our heads billowing from a window ledge.

Down side streets we stop,
In front of a nightclub
Sleeping in the sun,
Stoop for shade,
The clang of knives and forks echoes
In my ears.

A sparrow gives a quick flash of its wings
Before retreating to the rooftops.

Pavilion gardens, fragrant flowers in bloom,
Man busking, his hat empty.

Christopher Koutsoukos (11)
Carlton Hill Primary School, Brighton

What Can I See?

What can I see?
Fluffy clouds with legs,
Houses with straw roofs,
Washing hung up on pegs,
Horses with big hooves.

What can I feel?
A soft cool breeze,
That rustles through the trees,
The floorboards underneath my feet,
I feel scared about the people that I'll meet.

What can I hear?
Tractors cutting all the wheat,
My feet as I tap out a beat,
A creak when I walk on the floor,
The clunk when someone closed the door.

Caitlin Griffith (11)
Compton CE Primary School, Winchester

Thoughts Of An Evacuee

What can I feel?
I love my warm snuggly bed,
I feel the sweat running down my head
I feel nervous and unsteady,
Am I really, truly ready?

What do I hope for?
I hope the war will stop soon,
I hope for peace in the world,
Equal rights for different races,
I hope that Europe will be free.

What do I dream of?
I dream about days ahead.
I dream about my new family and the farm,
I dream of my mum and dad in London.
I dream that one day the war will be over.

Tom Jordan (11)
Compton CE Primary School, Winchester

What Can I . . . ?

What can I see?
Blue skies not a cloud in sight,
Green grass no more dusty roads,
Long stone roads as far as the eyes can see.
This is not how it used to be.

What can I feel?
A lump in my throat that tells me I should cry.
That heartbreaking moment when Mum said goodbye.
I feel the wind blowing on my young pale face,
I feel the calm of the blanket rubbing my face.

What can I hope for?
I hope for a world in peace,
The peace lasting for eternity,
So I can stay with my parents,
And not live in fear.

What can I dream of?
I dream of my mum.
I hope she misses me,
Just like I miss her.
My dad might miss me - but I doubt it.

Arthur Scott-Geddes (10)
Compton CE Primary School, Winchester

What Can I See?

What can I see?
I can see a field of cotton wool,
With little matchstick legs,
I can see a shelter which is filled with children and their name pegs,
I can see a river shining in the sun,
I hope I am going to have fun.

What can I feel?
I can feel my little sister,
While I scratch my painful blister,
I can feel a spider crawling up my leg,
I can feel my cosy blanket lying on my bed.

What can I hear?
I can hear the cotton wool balls bleating,
And their thundering hooves as they run,
I can hear the chatter of excited children and
The occasional howl of despair,
I can hear the rushing river running through the bright green field,
Now I am satisfied because I know I won't die.

Grace Allen (10)
Compton CE Primary School, Winchester

What Can I See?

What can I see?
A beautiful butterfly,
And a little buzzy bee,
Little white blobs,
And a bird in a tree.

What can I hear?
A creaking in the floorboard,
And a cow going moo,
Nothing else but silence,
Nothing here to do.

What can I feel?
The softness of my teddy,
And a tickle on my toes,
I feel a breaking in my heart,
Mum and I should never be apart.

What do I hope for?
I hope that the country is a big adventure
And the people I have are kind,
I hope that Mum could be here right now,
And both Mum and Dad are safe.

Florence Mannerings (9)
Compton CE Primary School, Winchester

What Can I See?

What can I see?
A bird and a bee
Everything's green
As green as a bean
The clouds have legs
And there are chickens that lay eggs
There are lots of fields
But no cars on wheels.

What can I hear?
A duck and a deer
The stomping of shoes
And cows going moo
The buzz of a fly
As it goes flying by.

What do I hope for?
The end of the war
To see Mum again
And lose all the pain
That's just how I want it to be.

Annie Green (10)
Compton CE Primary School, Winchester

Evacuee

What can I see?
Everything is green.
I see fields and grass.
I can't see cars,
I can see curtains flapping in the wind
But nothing else moves.

What do I feel?
I feel lonely and unwanted.
I don't know anyone.
I don't feel safe
I feel empty and lost.

What do I dream of?
I dream of the war ending.
I dream of seeing my family.
I dream of returning to my city.
I dream of peace in the world.

Clara Jordan (11)
Compton CE Primary School, Winchester

The Slate Quarry

What is the slate quarry anyway?
An ugly scar on the landscape,
Grey steps hewn out of the rock.

And what of the men who worked there?
The chip, chip, chip of metal on stone
Suspended on a rope, trusting the rope, what if it snaps?

What do the men do now?
Five years apprenticeship
Wasted on a bunch of tourists.

Tamara Stojanovic (11)
Dolphin School, Reading

Rainbow

Red is the warmth of Christmas morning,
With stockings full of presents.

Red is the anger of jealous men
With blood and broken hearts.

Red is the love of Valentine's Day
With hearts and mystery cards.

Orange is the flame of a burning house,
With screams and rising smoke.

Orange is a yummy carrot
That rabbits like to eat.

Yellow is the brightening sun,
That blinds you when you look at it.

Yellow is the summer flowers
And the colour of sour lemons.

Green is life of a jungle
With its leaves and peacefulness.

Green is 'to go' from a traffic light
That gives you speed and freedom.

Blue is the deep blue sea,
That reflects off the wondering sky.

Blue is bluebells
That rise in spring.

Indigo is a Cadbury's wrapper
Which you can smell the chocolate through.

Indigo is Mary, Jesus' mother
All the way up in Heaven.

Violet is the violets
That grow in summer gardens.

Violet are the chocolate creams
That my mummy likes to eat.

Samantha Green (10)
Dolphin School, Reading

Rainbow Poem

Red is war
Blood, guts and sadness
Oh all those poor wounded soldiers
Who fought in the Great War's madness.

Orange is like Tropicana
All sweet and juicy within.
It's also tigers and lions
With striped and spotted skins.

Yellow is homework diaries
Which is not a very good thing.
It's also lemons and daisies,
More delight for the world they bring.

Green is nature
Stems, leaves and grass
It's also the shade worn by soldiers
Who destroy this scene with a blast.

Blue is water
Channels, lakes and seas
It's also the colour worn by policemen
Who chase robbers and thieves.

Indigo is all sorts of flowers,
Pansies and violets are examples.
It's a colour that's often hard to describe,
But the sky at dusk must be sampled.

Of all the shades of the rainbow
Violet is the last.
It's hard to think of examples
So let's move on fast.

Edward Roberts (10)
Dolphin School, Reading

Rainbow Murder At Midnight

Red is the blood of a victim, it poured across the floor
Or the colour of the carpet, it's laid upon.
Red is their cheeks as they get ready for their last dance,
Or their heart pumping as they walk to the door.

Orange is the fear in their eyes as the murderer strikes,
Or the carrot in their last meal,
Orange is when your last sun sets,
Or your last look at the marigolds before you fade away.

Yellow, the final smile you give
Or the last buttercup you see bloom,
Yellow is summer turning away to let winter come
Or the canary flying past the striker coming for you.

Green is envy leaking out of your opponent
Or the colour in your voice as you fall,
Green, the jealousy pouring out of you as you die,
Or your withered hand beginning to rot.

Indigo, the dress you wore for your last step
Or the nightlight shining in,
Indigo, your face in the darkness,
Or the colour of day to night.

Violet, the ring on the finger about to fall,
Or the priest praying at my grave,
Violet, the shock to my relations
Or the flowers on my grave the next day.

Serenna Ferguson (9)
Dolphin School, Reading

Rainbow Poem

Red is Valentine's Day, heart-shaped cards
The colour of soldiers yelling
War and blood
Yet at the same time, the happiness of Christmas.

Orange is the colour of tangerines
Clementines that taste so good
Tasty and fresh when you bite into them
Orange is our source of light
Orange is the sun.

Yellow is the beautiful flowers
That open in the spring
Yellow is those fruity lemons
With a lovely scent.

Green is nature
Where the trees sway in the wind
The grass which slowly turns brown as people walk on it
Leaves which blow with the trees.

Blue is the day's sky,
Fogged with clouds but still lovely to look up at,
While you think
The sea which ripples in the wind.

Indigo is the night sky speckled with stars and planets,
Indigo is ink
So useful to everyone.

Alicia McDermott (10)
Dolphin School, Reading

Brrm Rustle, Brrm Chomp!

Mum says it's a blessing, others it's a curse
I say it's the place where Mum empties out her purse.

I think it's so silent, like voices never heard
My mum walks around, chatting like a nerd!

Waitrose, oh Waitrose, Waitrose come feed me
Waitrose, oh Waitrose, I'm begging for my tea!

The till bells started ringing, someone's in a rush,
Mum has gone to get, a box of strawberry crush.

Waitrose, oh Waitrose, Waitrose come feed me
Waitrose, oh Waitrose, I've still not got my tea!

Finally we are leaving, the sounds all fade away
Leaving this place of boredom, hip hip, hip hip, hooray!

The door creaks slowly open, peace for me at last
My sister's screaming voice, just hit me with a blast!

Waitrose, oh Waitrose, Waitrose you've fed me
Waitrose, oh Waitrose, I'm full of yummy tea!

Emily Dick-Cleland (10)
Dolphin School, Reading

Guts And Gore

Red is blood and guts and flesh seeping out of a wounded chest.

Orange is sickly stomach juice swirling out of a gunshot wound.

Yellow is churned and mashed up food that makes you rush
to the loo.

Green is a septic, raised up spot, if it bursts it will bleed a lot.

Blue is jelly seeping from an eye or an abandoned person left to die!

Indigo is a swollen, infected tongue, or a rotting mouldy piece of lung.

Violet is a pulsing vein, or a murdered man lying in a drain.

Mark Terry (10)
Dolphin School, Reading

Cwm Idwal

A dull grey day, the hard breeze whistling round and round
The sunlight twinkling behind the enormous giant-like mountains.
The lake glistening and gleaming into the eyes.
The clouds moving up above, as slow as snails.
The weak birds trying to defeat the wind.
But being blown down and down onto the earth.
The small streams flowing by our side
The heavy footsteps coming nearer and nearer.
The rock path, it felt hard on the feet
It looked strong and dark whilst trudging up them one by one.
The smells of the damp, dewy grass drifting past me.
The sound of the stream trickling by, entering my ears.
I feel the whistling wind swaying me this way and that way
The cold air was running through my veins
Suddenly the sun appeared from behind the monstrous mountains
The sun was shining, everything brightened, everything warmed.

Beth Glover (11)
Dolphin School, Reading

The Forest

Walking through the peaceful forest trying to be silent
Beautiful day, sun setting, every creature out of sight
Twigs snapping, bushes shaking as we trudge
Through bright, colourful rhododendrons with a beaming view.

Hopelessly trying to catch my breath
Struggling to get to the top
All I see is a pink and blue top to toe sky
Whilst lying down on the star moss.

Listening while resting, closing my eyes
Hearing an amazing song played by the birds
The cool, gentle breeze of the night
All of it sweeps me off my feet, through the forest I walk.

Holly Janes (11)
Dolphin School, Reading

A Rainbow Poem

Red is summer fruits
With redcurrants, cherries and more.

Orange is a warning
Telling you to stop.

Yellow is for sunshine
Showing you the way.

Green is the emerald
Glinting in the light.

Blue is for the sea
Splashing on the shore.

Indigo is a berry
From which dye is plentiful.

Violet is for violets
Dancing in the sun.

Anais King (10)
Dolphin School, Reading

The Castle

Framed on a hilltop,
Moonlight shining through broken battlements,
Impressive, intimidating,
Remembering the souls of those who lived there,
Over a thousand years deceased,
Enforcing lost memories,
Battles, wars and bloodshed,
Its sinister frame,
Imprisoning forgotten recollections of hard times past,
The castle, malevolent and threatening.

Sophie Utting (11)
Dolphin School, Reading

Child's Birthday Party

Singing Happy Birthday,
I don't like the sound
Ripping off the paper
My cat scared of the crowd.

It's not very quiet,
It's really rather loud,
I can't bear the noise,
I'll have to go outside.

Popping of the big balloons
Screaming children running round
It's so very frantic
And hard to explain the sound.

The party's almost over,
Thank you God for that
Another year to wait
Until my sister's eight.

Trixie Roddick (10)
Dolphin School, Reading

The Walk To The Bewilderness

It was getting darker and darker
Time was precious as the sky was getting darker
For some people it was harder to see
We turned round and headed back
The group took a detour and we went down
A very steep slope down and down until
We got back.

Anton Capstack (11)
Dolphin School, Reading

Sounds Spooky

The mournful moaning
Of a guitar
Rung in the ears of the
Drunk Reading crowd.

Onto the cliff
Where the wind singer sings
On the top of the peak
Where the death bell rings.

The bright silver moon
Shone in the sky
With an owl's hooting
And a werewolf's cry.

The creaking of the floorboard
The purring of a cat
The groaning of the bed springs
And the scraping of a mat.

The daybreak of the morning
The burning of the fire
The blackened ashes
Left behind to die.

Alex Hall (9)
Dolphin School, Reading

Cwm

You are a mountain corrie,
Peaceful, quiet, windy.
Like a leaf long and flat you sit.
Your colour is not happy but not sad.
Your colour is, for those who sit there, calm.
Once you held gallons of ice
That ripped you clear.
A big, though pleasant cwm
You will always be there.

Alex Morgan (11)
Dolphin School, Reading

Beddgelert

Arriving at the beautiful Beddgelert,
You might think all these cars would ruin it
But the tourists just want to pay their respect.

Beddgelert, Beddgelert,
How pretty you are.

They pay their respect to the poor slain dog
Walking through the countryside,
Thinking about . . .

Beddgelert, Beddgelert,
How pretty you are.

Gelert the dog was a normal wolfhound
Gelert the dog did nothing at all.
Gelert the dog saved a life.
Little did he know it was in return for his.

Beddgelert, Beddgelert,
How pretty you are.

Beddgelert, Beddgelert,
You do amazing ice cream
Beddgelert, Beddgelert,
The best I've ever had.

Beddgelert, Beddgelert,
How pretty you are.

Jade Savage (11)
Dolphin School, Reading

Cwm

C wm, you sit alone, no one to talk to.
W ind ruffles your waters.
M ountains around you, grey and still.

Marko Stojanovic (11)
Dolphin School, Reading

A Walk In The Welsh Woods

The wind whispers to the trees
Making their sage leaves shake
The wind whistles down from the mountain
Rippling over the lake.

The shadows dance across the floor
Dappling the emerald carpet with stars
Casting a spell across the forest
Free of the noise of people and cars.

The piercing call of a nightingale
Like a piccolo over a crowd
Echoing in my eardrums
A clear and beautiful sound.

Flowers of dazzling brightness
Speckling the floor like sparks
A bird calls over the music of the wind
A shrill goodnight from a lark.

Sophie Eager (11)
Dolphin School, Reading

Caernarfon

Caernarfon Castle towers over you
Making you feel small and insignificant
Unfinished but not ruined.
Beddgelert or Gelert's Grave
The legend of a dog carved in stone.
Beaumaris Moat, the ducklings swim past
Scurrying after their mother,
The cygnets glide along the lake
As if with no effort at all.
We sit and sketch the high walls
Marvelling at the beauty all around.

Ema Stojanovic (11)
Dolphin School, Reading

The Big Match

Climbing down the stairs
Looking for our seats
We are on Row 21
But where on Earth could it be?

The big match about to start
We're all excited before
The starting whistle about to blow
Toot toot, there it goes.

The sound of the ball hitting the bar
And the cheers within
The Liverpool song about to start
Oh my gosh, I need to sing.

'We love you Liverpool' we sang,
And the opposition about to too
The sound of the hotdog seller
Man, I need some food.

The sound of Morientes striking the ball,
Whoosh! What a goal!
We all cheer with glee
Then we all go marching home
Happy as can be.

Dheeraj Ahluwalia (9)
Dolphin School, Reading

Cwm

Alive with life
Unspoilt by man
Tranquil and soundless
The river white and moving rapidly
So pretty to the eye
Green and yellow
The cwm where the ice settled
It was created 10,000 years ago
Scoured by ice.

Evan Richardson (11)
Dolphin School, Reading

Beaumaris Castle

It was pretty, ivy crawling up the side,
The sea breeze rustling the trees,
With its small dock, right up to the wall,
The towering gate and towers,
The beautiful glistening moat,
With four cute ducklings,
Trapped inside the two curtained walls.
Feel as if you will be shot.
Wander round and round trying to get in.
Go inside all the towers,
Pretend to fire an arrow,
Through a narrow slit,
Inside a huge great hall.
A bright white painted chapel
Hear in your mind the angels singing
Into all the winding corridors and passages.
Up to where King Edward listened to musicians
He liked the soft sweet sound of the harp best.
See the huge oven inside the ancient kitchen.
Next, the amazing view of the sea
The rolling hills on the mainland,
Feel scared but somehow joyful,
This is Beaumaris Castle.

Imogen Hay (11)
Dolphin School, Reading

Harlech

H arlech Castle, a castle overlooking the sea.
A lookout post for the soldiers.
R eaching to the top of the sky
L ying on top of the rock.
E nding enemies' lives at its walls
C ourtyard with stone buildings
H arlech Castle.

Daleep Singh (10)
Dolphin School, Reading

The Quiet Countryside!

Oh! The peaceful countryside
Hears a cow *moo!*
Ooh how blasting
The car skidding round the bend.

Oh! The peaceful countryside
Hear a tractor mowing the hay
Very noisy
The car skidding round the bend.

Oh! The peaceful countryside
Bang! Bang! A man shooting a pheasant
What a racket
The car skidding round the bend.

Oh! The peaceful countryside
Hear the horse *neigh! Neigh!*
How deafening
The car skidding round the bend.

Oh! The peaceful farm
Hear the animals, *Moo! Neigh! Baa! Bang!*
Woof! Miaow!
What a noisy ear-spitting racket
While the car headed up the quiet city
No sound to be heard.

Charlie Corcoran (10)
Dolphin School, Reading

The Electric Mountain

The electric mountain was huge
Towering like a skyscraper
With all the pipes running in and out like snakes
The inside tunnels lined with concrete like a great suit of armour.

It generated electricity fast like a horse in a race
The halls were vast like a desert plane
But it was as cold as winter.

Aran McGroarty (11)
Dolphin School, Reading

The Kitchen

The clanging of pots
The rattle of spoons
Sounds like a bad music song.

The banging of drawers
The rumbling of the mixer
Sounds like an Arctic storm.

The sizzle of fat
The splash of the tap
Sounds like a blind man in an antique store.

The chopping of the knife
The trickle of vinegar
Sounds like the wind on glass.

The trickle of the coffee machine
The crackling of the gas oven
Sounds like my mum in the kitchen.

Emily Bonsor (10)
Dolphin School, Reading

Nant Ffrancon

Intimidated I stand alone,
Gazing, gazing,
At the vast valley below me.
Unimaginable,
Unthinkable.
One kilometre of ice,
Stretching to the highest peak,
Small, jutting out summits,
Imagination.

Joshua Weekly (11)
Dolphin School, Reading

Farm In The Morning

Early in the morning if you come across a farm,
Stop and listen carefully, to all the different sounds.

Dogs barking, *yap, yap,*
Cats crying, *miaow,*
Chickens always clucking, *cluck*
Horses in the barn.

Ducks squawking, *quack, quack,*
Cows mooing, *moo*
Sheep baaing all the time
Crows calling, *coo.*

Pigs snorting, *oink, oink*
Goats want their food
Donkeys braying, *aay-ore*
Geese in a mood.

The farmyard is silent, too quiet to be true,
Until the cockerel cries at dawn, *cock-a-doodle-doo!*

Charlotte Smith (9)
Dolphin School, Reading

Ice Cream At Beddgelert

B rown chocolate ice cream melting in my mouth
E very day melting in my mouth
D own from the cone the ice cream goes
D ipping in a flake of chocolate
G reat, gorgeous taste
E normous scoops of ice cream
L ick, lick, lick
E veryone licks, licks, licks
R umbling through their tummy
T asty, wonderful.

William Barnard (10)
Dolphin School, Reading

Dissonance

The blast of a shattering bomb so hideous,
A rattling machine gun, so deadly and furious,
Thunderous sounds of a storm, so *injurious*.
Adult issues so deep, boring and serious.
The screeching of a bird so loud and shrill,
The monotonous whine of a dentist's drill,
The bullet shooting, wanting to kill,
Leave me feeling profoundly ill.

But a lullaby, so sweet and dear,
Joyous laughter, so full of cheer,
A mother's voice, caring and sincere,
Cleanses my mind of worry and fear.
The sound of frolicking children in the sand,
The vibrant music of an inspired band,
The excited clapping of a person's hand,
What more in life could you demand?

Daniel Hallstrom (10)
Dolphin School, Reading

The Story Of Beddgelert

B eautiful village to walk around in.
E xtremely yummy ice cream for us to eat.
D ifferent flavours of ice cream, scrummy in our tummies.
D readful story of Gelert the dog, made us sad.
G elert's grave was much older than my great, great Grandad.
E njoyed Beddgelert like you would too!
L itter was nowhere as clean as Buckingham Palace.
E xciting village survey, to had fun doing.
R apid river running through the village.
T he prince and his wife had a wolfhound dog and a baby boy.

Jemma Guile (11)
Dolphin School, Reading

Slate Quarry

The stiff stingy smell still lies in the walls
The layers upon layers they broke
The adventure of walking along their treasure,
To see how they lived.
Mining the slate.
Not even for themselves, but for the bosses.
Rations on the amount they could buy
Cold, dreary winter, lasting for months ahead.
Their cold fingers turning blue as they hammer away.
The hammering,
The pain,
The knocking,
No gain.
The money they earnt would be enough for a loaf of bread to share.

Stephanie Babb (10)
Dolphin School, Reading

Child's Birthday Party

What I can hear
Is a very noisy sound
Screaming of the children
All playing on the ground.

The balloons are all popping
And the music's very loud
They're singing Happy Birthday
Round a cake to make her proud.

She's blowing out the candles
The party poppers start
A girl is sitting, crying
Little sweetheart.

Ellie Roberts (9)
Dolphin School, Reading

The Colours Of The Rainbow

Red is the colour of flames that sit in our fireplace.
It is the colour of blood and a broken heart.

Orange is the fruit that we eat every day.

Yellow is the colour of the sun that shines on us all day long.
It is the colour of butter we spread on our toast.
It is the colour of custard that we pour on our apple crumble.

Green is the colour of leaves that fall off trees.

Blue is the colour of the sky that is above us.
It is the colour of the sea where dolphins flick their tails.

Indigo is the colour of the sky when the sun sets.

Violet is the flower that is in our garden.

Lucy Lowe (9)
Dolphin School, Reading

A Mountain Call

No human call echoes through the icy slopes
But the mountains were far from silent,
Tiny birds called their greetings
In a number of quiet chirps.
Larger birds made occasional but louder calls,
That hung in the air for minutes.
A mountain goat galloped across the bumpy ground
Its hooves made soft clip-clopping noises
The sharp, cold wind whistled
Through the barren land.

Eva Steinhardt (10)
Dolphin School, Reading

My Poem of Rainbows

Red is crimson with war, with blood and guts of enemies and
friends flying
Red is love and scarlet roses blooming.

Orange is the amber that insects got stuck in years and years ago
Orange is the flame in the hearth of a cottage.

Yellow is lemon zest bubbling in a pot
Yellow is the joy and happiness of children playing in the sun.

Green is the grass with moss on in the morning
Green is the waters of the sea which the fish swim in.

Blue is the rain that beats down upon plants, flowers, and herbs.
Blue is the sea which rolls onto the beach with foamy waves.

Indigo is the sky at night, when the moon is full and the stars
are bright.

Violet is the lavender and violets of summer.

Octavia Pearce (10)
Dolphin School, Reading

The Silence

I am standing here in solemn silence
My stomach's churning with suspense
Hoping to hear just one single sound
Like the patter of paws on wet, muddy ground
Or the flap of a bird as he opens his wings,
Or the squawk of that bird as he starts to sing
I'm hoping to hear just one single sound
Like the patter of paws on wet, muddy ground.
But standing there listening as hard as I could
Not one single sound did I hear in that wood.

Beatrice Clegg (10)
Dolphin School, Reading

Rainbow Football Poem

Red is Liverpool FC who are the best
Red is Arsenal FC who are just rubbish
Red is Man U which is a word that shouldn't be said
Red is England who are our international team.

Orange is Holland who are an international team
Orange is Ipswich away who are in the Championship
Orange is Bristol Rovers away who aren't very good
Orange is Albacete who are a Spanish team.

Yellow is Norwich who are getting relegated
Yellow is Brazil who are an international team
Yellow is Liverpool away who are just the best
Yellow is Club Brugge who aren't very good.

Green is Ireland who are an international team
Green is Sporting Lisbon who are a Portuguese team
Green is Celtic who are a Scottish team
Green is Porto away who are a Portuguese team.

Blue is Chelsea who aren't too good
Blue is Blackburn who are a disgrace to football
Blue is Birmingham who are outrageously bad
Blue is Porto who are foreigners.

Indigo is Barca (striped) who Stephen hates
Indigo is Crystal Palace (striped) who are ridiculous
Indigo is Basel (striped) who no one has heard of
I don't know another indigo team.

No violet teams exist so I will end the poem here
Thank you for reading it.

Alex Dilley (9)
Dolphin School, Reading

Colours

Red is the symbol of danger with arrows rushing through the air.
Red is the colour of blood when people die in hard battles.
Red are the roses swaying in your back garden.
Red is the symbol for Red Nose Day when people wearing
Red noses all laugh happily.
Red is the heart on Valentines cards you send and receive on
the 14th February.

Orange is the fruit you eat during or after a match.
Orange is the sunset that happens when the sun goes down.
Orange is the colour of the marigolds swaying in the gentle breeze.

Yellow is the colour of a banana, you munch on during the day.
Yellow is the colour of the sun blowing down on a hot day.
Yellow is butter you spread on your potatoes at dinner time.
Yellow is custard you pour on your apple tart.

Green is the colour of leaves that fall onto the green grass.
Green is the colour of my favourite grapes I like to eat.
Green is the colour of the beans that wind their way up their
beanpoles.
Green is the colour of a freshly mown lawn you can play lots of
games on.

Blue is the colour of the sky with clouds racing across it.
Blue is the colour of the sea with fish swimming in and out.
Blue is the colour of water dripping out of taps.

Indigo is the night sky when lights go off in people's houses.

Violet is the wrapping of a Cadbury's Dairy Milk chocolate bar.
Violet is the flower glistening in the sunlight.

Stephanie Wright (10)
Dolphin School, Reading

Rainbow Dream

Red
Red is a fire on a cold winter's night
Red is the anger of a half-eaten strawberry
Red is a heart of blood that's beating all day long.

Orange
Orange is a fruit that gives you vitamins and minerals
Orange is the sun in the sky.

Yellow
Yellow is a lemon that grows on a tree
Yellow is a buttercup that shows under your chin as yellow.

Green
Green is a leaf that falls in autumn
Green is an olive that you eat for snacks
Green is a growth of ivy that grows upon a wall.

Blue
Blue is the sky high up in the clouds
Blue is the sea that is rocking.

Indigo
Indigo is the sun setting in the sky
Indigo is a tulip in the garden.

White
White is all the rainbow colours put together.

Lily Thomas (10)
Dolphin School, Reading

Colour Poem

Red is blood, which happens in the war.
Red is the happiness of Christmas, Santa and his sleigh.
Red happens at Valentine's Day, chocolates and cards.
Red is a strange colour but I like it just the same.

Orange is fruity, oranges and mango.
Orange comes at Hallowe'en, pumpkins and witches too.
Orange is the marigolds, which bloom in the summer
Orange is great, it's a happy colour.

Yellow is the sun, on a nice bright day
Yellow is lemony and *bananary* too.
Yellow is the scent of flowers, buttercups and dandelions.
Yellow is a pretty colour but onto the next one now.

Green is holly which grows on the bushes,
Green is olives and cucumber which you eat most days.
Green is grassy and leaves of trees which fall in autumn.
Green is everywhere, you cannot lose it.

Blue is the sky, so beautiful, so clear.
Blue is swimming pools, where people play each day.
Blue is blueberries and bluebells
Blue is a nice colour just like you.

Indigo is the night sky, when the stars are up high.
Indigo is the pretty pansy you are wanting to touch
Indigo's around, but there's not very much.

Violet are flowers, violets and lavender
Violet are tasty grapes.
Violet is a girl's bedroom wall and her purply dress
Violet's the last colour of the rainbow.

Anna McMurtrie (10)
Dolphin School, Reading

Jealousy

Jealousy, I could go to the Devil with it.
Jealousy, stuck in my mind, banging on my forehead.
Thunder starts to fall from my dark and gloomy mind.
Why can't I be like her? Nice.
With long legs and pointy boots
Unlike me with soggy trainers.
No long hair down to the middle of my back.
Hatred in my blustery skull.
All I want is to grow longer hair.
Be just like her.
Maybe I will turn out like her.
It does run in the family!

Alex Childs (9)
Inkpen Primary School, Hungerford

Happiness

Happiness has come to stay.
It sits next to me singing lovely songs.
Sweet soft ones on my bed.
I went to reach out to him
But he zooms away like a shooting star.
It is cheerful every minute and every hour.

Kerry Faulkner (9)
Inkpen Primary School, Hungerford

Jealousy

Jealousy is something dark and solid
Easily caused.
It looks like darkness.
Beware! It takes over your mind.
Jealousy will persuade you to do
Something terrible.
Once you're jealous, you're stuck with it.

Lloyd Childs (11)
Inkpen Primary School, Hungerford

Joy

Joy, it is skipping around my room.
It's loud and likes to sing lots of jiggy music.
Yellow, cuddly, I like to squeeze it tight in my arms.
As he prances around the room he brightens everything.
Everything I see now is cheerful.

Joy, it has come to stay.
It makes me want to join in.
Staring out of the window with bright blue eyes.
At night it sleeps peacefully on my bed.

Lucy Dodridge (11)
Inkpen Primary School, Hungerford

Anger

Anger makes my head bulge
Is red with bloodshot eyes
Talking to himself loud and bold
Making me pour with rain
Sleeping under my bed day after day
Giving me a red face with frustration.

Conor Hurst (10)
Inkpen Primary School, Hungerford

Anger

Anger has come to stay. I wish it hadn't.
It looks ready to strike at me.
Screaming on the end of my bed
Like a red fireball.
Rough and bumpy
Very vicious and mean.

Max Butterworth (9)
Inkpen Primary School, Hungerford

Frustration

Frustration, it has come to stay,
It's black, dull and spiky.
Nothing goes my way,
I never do anything right
Because of it
Living in my cupboard.

It's the end of the world,
I know it.
I wish I could slap it,
Lock it away.
I've tried; it doesn't work.

I become hot and clammy,
My heart pumps faster,
My head works faster.
Why me?
Why not her or him?
It's not fair!
It's stuck with me forever!

Amy Hooper (11)
Inkpen Primary School, Hungerford

Happiness

Happiness has come to stay.
It starts to dance when I turn the music on,
Smooth and blue, its shape is a circle
Two eyes and a big shiny mouth.

Happiness has come to stay,
It's sitting at the end of my bed.
Brings happiness all around
But slowly it rolls away.

I will miss it . . .

Hannah Warrick (11)
Inkpen Primary School, Hungerford

Birds

They hatch in their nests,
They screech all day,
They need their food,
To catch their prey.
Baby birds.

Hawks hovering in the air
Swooping down to catch its prey,
Gliding in the warm thermals,
Enjoying a bright spring day.

Finches twitter on the wooden post,
Birds bathe so brave and bold,
Winter water freezing cold,
Robin redbreast hunts his worm.

They hatch in their nest,
Hawks hovering in the air,
Finches twitter on the wooden post,
All different birds.

Jack Henry Bailey-Bale (10)
Inkpen Primary School, Hungerford

Love

Love, it has come to stay,
It waltzes through my body.
Pink and red, as fluffy as a thousand feathers.
Love has a soft and gentle voice.

Alix Wiltshire (10)
Inkpen Primary School, Hungerford

Girl

She stared in windows, in mirrors,
In puddles,
And there was a sickly reflection.

No one was there.

She trundled round day and night,
She trundled round in black and white,
Although she knew it would do no good.

No one was there.

She felt like she was being pulled on puppet strings,
Pulling and pushing round in circles.
Again she looked in her reflection.

No one was there.

She stared in windows, in mirrors,
In puddles as if it was wrong,
She turned to see her reflection.
There wasn't one.

And people were in plight,
Trying to recognise her,
Still she saw them in black and white.

No one was there.

To go,
To fly,
With the wink of one's eye.

No one was there.

She stared in windows, in mirrors,
In puddles as if it was wrong,
She turned to see her reflection.

This time she was gone.

Holly Titford (11)
Inkpen Primary School, Hungerford

A 2 Z Of Animals

A is for animals
B is for bumblebees
C is for cats and Sassy is her name
D is for dogs who like to bark
E is for elephant with a big trunk
F is for frogs who live in the pond
G is for goats who have a long beard
H is for horses who are quick
I is for insects
J is for jungles with cool animals
K is for king of the jungle
L is for leopards who are tree climbers
M is for monkeys who are cheeky
N is for newts who swim in the pond
O is for octopuses who swim in the sea
P is for pigs who play in the mud
Q is for quails who sing all day
R is for rabbits who like to nibble
S is for sharks who like to kill
T is for tigers who pounce on their prey
U is for unicorns who gallop through the trees
V is for vultures who fly around
W is for walrus who have big tusks
X is for x-rays that vets use
Y is for yaks who have lots of fun
Z is for zebras who have stripes.

Kimberley Johnson (9)
Inkpen Primary School, Hungerford

Falcon

Swiftly drifting down,
Rising upwards gracefully,
Talons ready to seize its prey.

Adrian Wells (11)
Inkpen Primary School, Hungerford

The Magic Box

(Based on 'Magic Box' by Kit Wright)

I will put in the box . . .
The swish of a lion's mane in a summer's night breeze.
Fire from an evil devil laughing at people in pain.
The tip of a child's twitchy toe touching water.

I will put in the box . . .
A snowman with an icy frozen heart.
A sip from a glass of freshly made milk.
A leaping leopard racing for its petrified prey.

I will put in the box . . .
Three frightened pigs from a fairy tale.
The last living elegant eagle soaring through the spectacular sky.
And the first juicy apple touching a young boy's lips.

I shall sit on my lion's back
Dodging all the low branches as he speeds under towering trees.
Then watch him tear up a helpless victim with his cruel claws.

Richard Butler (11)
Kempshott Junior School, Basingstoke

What Is Blue?

Blue is the colour of the glowing neon lights
Underneath a huge hammer.

Blue is the colour of the beam of Anakin's light sabre
Smouldering Count Dooko's hand.

Blue is a big blueberry bath bomb
Fizzing and fizzing releasing its essence
To fill your bath with the scent of blueberry.

Blue smells like freshly cut mint
Sprinkled over luscious lamb roast.

Will Smith (11)
Kempshott Junior School, Basingstoke

The Magic Box

(Based on 'Magic Box' by Kit Wright)

I will put in the box . . .
The swish of an eagle's wing in the starry night sky.
Fire from a phoenix burning every house as it goes by.
The tip of a cat's nose as it makes its way through the muddy ditch.

I will put in the box . . .
A snowman on top of a shining star melting faster than
the speed of light.
A sip of the Nile's breath on the tip of your tongue.
A leaping grasshopper making its way through the massive
long grass.

I will put in the box . . .
Three golden magical wishes spoken in French.
The last breath of a dying dragon
And the first word to keep my friends all together.

Ashley Brown (11)
Kempshott Junior School, Basingstoke

Green

Green smells like the freshly cut grass lying in a meadow.
Green sounds like a greenfly zooming around like a mini aeroplane.
Green is a leaf floating down from a huge oak tree.
Green feels like lush grass on our school field, can you see?
Green is our chairs that we sit on during the day.
Green is a colour that makes you shout 'hooray!'
Green is a calm colour, well I think that.
Green is my Peugeot 206 where I sat.
Green tastes like yummy salad that I ate for my dinner.
If we had a poem competition, I would be the winner.
So green is a lovely colour, as you can see,
I like the colour green lots, well that's only me.

Stuart Locke (10)
Kempshott Junior School, Basingstoke

The Magic Box

(Based on 'Magic Box' by Kit Wright)

I will put in the box . . .
The swish of fresh rippling water trickling down from the
Tip of a mountain.
Fire from the black coal giving warmth to a family on a winter's chill.
The tip of spring filling the world with carnivals of colours
And a party of smell.

I will put in the box . . .
A snowman made with love, affection and happiness
A sip of untouched and unpolluted water flowing down your throat,
Refreshing you,
A leaping spark from an energetic child.

I will put in the box . . .
Three whispers of pain, death and cruelty,
The last cries of a quiet soul
And the first precious moments of a child's first steps.

I will put in the box . . .
A second moon watching over the Earth,
A mouse chasing a cat and a dog chasing the mouse.

My box is made from gold, stars and happiness with hope on the lid,
And whispers in the corners,
The hinges are butterflies making the box open and close,
I shall glide on my box over the diamond crystal moon,
Then wash up on a golden beach, the colour of a queen's crown.

Hannah Ulysses (11)
Kempshott Junior School, Basingstoke

The Magic Box

(Based on 'Magic Box' by Kit Wright)

I will put in the box . . .
The swish of a bright flag billowing in the north wind
Marking the end of a terrible time.
Fire from the centre of the core of the Earth.
The tip of Mount Kilimanjaro, ancient and resting.

I will put in the box . . .
A snowman that has survived summer
A sip of melted silver cast into the depths of a star.
A leaping laugh sprung from the centre of your heart.

I will put in the box . . .
Three joys, three sorrows and three fates
The last thought of a soul that is just about to be sent to Heaven,
And the first thought of the Earth's life.

I will put in the box . . .
A second summer and a tenth planet
A man with wings and a bird with arms.

My box is fashioned from ice and fire and light and dark,
Each sprung from the depths of the Earth.
With hope on the top and depression in the corners.
The hinges are made of the most magical bylines shining 24 hours
a day.
I shall surf on my box on the volcanic lava deep below the centre
of the Earth.
Then I will relax on the biggest glazier in the North Pole,
And glide away in my dreams on that magic box.

Thomas Quayle (11)
Kempshott Junior School, Basingstoke

The Magic Box

(Based on 'Magic Box' by Kit Wright)

I will put in the box . . .
The swish of the cat's tail as it runs into the distance.
Fire from the burning eyes of a camel.
The tip of a tongue licking precious lips.

I will put in the box . . .
A snowman with a cold carrot nose
A sip of the clearest sea in the land
A leaping spark from a burning fire.

I will put in the box . . .
Three colourful rainbows sitting in the sky
The last tear of a child as it leaves its mother
And the first miaow of a cat as it comes into the world.

I will put in the box . . .
A thirteenth month and a black moon
A cat on the bed
And a human on the floor.

My box is fashioned from silver and metal with moons on the lid,
And whispers in every corner.
Its hinges are finger joints of monsters.
I shall hike in my box
On the great height of the mountain
Then collapse on the mountain tops
The colour of the clouds.

Rhiann Sallows (11)
Kempshott Junior School, Basingstoke

The Magic Box

(Based on 'Magic Box' by Kit Wright)

I will put in my box . . .
The swish of a sleek sarong being handmade.
Fire from the stove on a snowy winter's day.
The tip of nature touching petrifying pollution.

I will put in my box . . .
A snowman sweating in the first vision of sun.
A sip of ice running down a steep sorry mountain.
A leaping lion cub playing with his elders.

I will put in my box . . .
Three precious stars, one for joy, one for love and one for happiness.
The last cries from a dying child,
And the first words of a baby heard by its mother.

I will put in my box . . .
A second winner with a gorgeous smile
A toddler at work writing all day
An adult at play loving every day.

My box is lined with silver and gold
With smiles in corners, and a lid of bows
Hinges made out of silk and satin.

I shall ride in my box
To the end of the long universe
Then discover aliens and the sweet little souls of happiness,
Joy, love and playfulness.

Lauren James (11)
Kempshott Junior School, Basingstoke

The Magic Box

(Based on 'Magic Box' by Kit Wright)

I will put in the box . . .
The swish of the silent wind in the calm of the night.
Fire burning then breathing out smoke.
The tip of a tree reaching out to the clouds.

I will put in the box . . .
A snowman melting a waving goodbye to life.
A sip of life's water kissing the cold lips of death.
A leaping leopard cub stretching for its mother.

I will put in the box . . .
Three broken hearts searching for new love
The last animal to leave the Earth
And the first blink of a baby in its mother's arms.

I will put in the box . . .
The thirteenth month of the year
A rose with a face
And a human with a rose expression.

My box is dressed with a golden coat
With jewels on the lid, promises in the corners.
Its hinges are the petals of an unknown plant.
I shall ice-skate in my box on the Arctic sea,
Meeting beautiful creatures, the colour of a rainbow.

Zoe Comerford (11)
Kempshott Junior School, Basingstoke

The Magic Box

(Based on 'Magic Box' by Kit Wright)

I will put in my box . . .
The swish of a lion warning of its predator
Fire from the eyes of an angry charging rhino
The tip of a sharp diamond like a star shimmering in the night sky.

I will put in my box . . .
A snowman with a melting heart, crying with pain.
A sip of ice-cold water making you feel warm inside.
A leaping kangaroo trying to find her young.

I will put in the box . . .
Three wishes from deep in my heart
The last tadpole in the pond, waiting until it turns into a frog
And the first smile of a newborn dragon.

I will put in the box . . .
A thirteenth month and a magical flower
A butterfly with two arms
And a human with antennae.

My box is made with kindness and peace
With love on the lid and painful secrets in the corners.
Its hinges are the muscles of a massive killer whale.
I shall bury my box, so nobody can see all of my secrets,
Then in fifty years time I will dig up my box
And release all of my great secrets into the world.

Amy Steel (11)
Kempshott Junior School, Basingstoke

The Magic Box

(Based on 'Magic Box' by Kit Wright)

I will put in the box . . .
The swish of a silken violet on a bright summer's day,
Fire from the Great Fire of London on Pudding Lane,
The tip of God's fingers touching mine.

I will put in the box . . .
A snowman with a frozen nose,
A sip from a kissing waterfall,
A leaping wave, the first one.

I will put in my box . . .
Three first raindrops that fall to Earth,
The last heartbeat of an extinct dodo,
And the kiss of a man and woman.

I will put in the box . . .
A fifth friend from a high mountain,
A cat with a dog's head and a dog with a cat's head.

My box has light from a desert moon and colours as bright
As a butterfly.
Shooting stars plucked out of the sky to hold the box together.

I shall walk in my box through the dusty moonlight,
And arrive at a sunny landscape.

Hayley Moore (11)
Kempshott Junior School, Basingstoke

What Is Pink?

Pink is marshmallows teasing you
Waiting to be eaten.
Pink is candyfloss melting on your tongue.
Pink is strawberry milkshake tingling your throat as you sip it slowly.
Pink is sweets! A child's dream!
Pink is the smell of sweet pollen on a spring flower.
Pink is happy, excited, soft and loving.

Chloe Udal (10)
Kempshott Junior School, Basingstoke

The Magic Box

(Based on 'Magic Box' by Kit Wright)

I will put in the box . . .
The swish of the sun steaming the ocean blue planet.
Fire from the exploding volcano as it rushes out.
The tip of the grass trying to survive as it reaches over to the
puddle of water.

I will put in the box . . .
A snowman crying icicle tears,
A sip from a waterfall as it rushes past,
A leaping dolphin as it skims over the frozen water.

I will put in the box . . .
Three shimmering stars sitting in the sky,
The last smile of a tiger as it leaves its mother
And the first smile of a tiger as it is being born.

Olivia White (11)
Kempshott Junior School, Basingstoke

The Magic Box

(Based on 'Magic Box' by Kit Wright)

I will put in the box . . .
The swish of a falcon gliding on a summer breeze.
Fire from a rocket taking off to explore Mercury.
The tip of an astronaut's foot landing on a rocky moon.

I will put in the box . . .
A snowman freezing on a snowy day,
A sip of an ice cube melting in the mouth.
A leaping salmon trying to escape to an unfrozen lake.

I will put in the box . . .
Three special wishes that will never blow away
The last piece of schoolwork I have ever done,
And the first time my baby brother opened his eyes.

Scott Coomber (11)
Kempshott Junior School, Basingstoke

The Magic Box

(Based on 'Magic Box' by Kit Wright)

The swish of an eagle's wings swooping in on its prey,
Fire from a blazing fire warming the house,
The tip of a star point twinkling in the night sky.

I will put in the box . . .
A snowman, as frozen, as an ice cube, standing still,
A sip of the finest water found in a well,
A leaping frog bouncing to its heart's content.

I will put in the box . . .
Three precious gems found in a crate of gold,
The last flake of snow which fell in the cold winter
And the first drop of rain that ever fell.

I will put in the box . . .
A fifth candle lit on Christmas Eve,
A picture of my family to remind me where I belong,
A spark from my eye when a picture is taken.

My box is smothered in a carpet of snow,
With a picture of me in the middle and my thoughts in the corners,
The sides are plaited from the dearest cotton.
I shall sail in the gold-dyed water with the rippling waves
As smooth as a river,
I will pick up my family
And let them share the happiness I feel.

Guy Pope (11)
Kempshott Junior School, Basingstoke

The Magic Box

(Based on 'Magic Box' by Kit Wright)

I will put in my box . . .
The swish of a mighty raven's wings, zooming for hours at night,
Fire from the hottest volcano in the giant universe,
As its pointy tip rapidly explodes, as it violently erupts.

I will put in my box . . .
A boiling snowman melting in the sun's waters,
Gushing aimlessly in its careless core,
A sip of the deadliest drink ever made,
A shouting spark, screaming at four ancient words,
Yet to be born.

I will put in my box . . .
Three gods of hatred, speaking their names in Arabic.
The last drip from a bleeding heart and the first death ever.

I will put in my box . . .
A sixty-first second and a black river,
A robin eating a dragon and a dragon eating a planet.

My box has no colour, you can see through it.
It is made out of ivory from a mammoth,
And it has no shape or size.

I shall die in my box, on the Earth's grave
Then go to Hades in triumph for evermore.

Mark Nickell (10)
Kempshott Junior School, Basingstoke

The Magic Box

(Based on 'Magic Box' by Kit Wright)

I will put in the box . . .
A swish of a golden silk scarf on a winter evening,
Fire from an angry man blowing his fuse,
The tip of the grass soothing my weary feet.

I will put in the box . . .
A snowman with a broken heart,
A sip of hope warming up a dinosaur,
A leap of a grasshopper jumping dramatically.

I will put in the box . . .
Three cheering football supporters cheering on their team,
The last Samari slitting someone's throat
And the first yawn of a baby leopard.

I will hide my box in my heart, waiting for my secrets to be revealed.
I will make my box of true secrets and thoughts the colour of love!

Sophie Webb (11)
Kempshott Junior School, Basingstoke

The Magic Box

(Based on 'Magic Box' by Kit Wright)

I will put in the box . . .
The swish of the purple velvet of the night sky,
Fire from the scalding heat of a infernal volcano,
The tip of a blue flame rising through the sky.

I will put in the box . . .
A snowman desperately fighting for its life,
A sip of a newborn creation somewhere far away,
A leaping scorpion in the vanishing desert.

I will put in the box . . .
Three delicate magical wishes spoken in gaelic,
The last shameful regret of a mass murderer,
And the jovial touch of a young funny girl.

Elliot Bateman (11)
Kempshott Junior School, Basingstoke

What Is Pink?

Pink is the colour of my lip gloss,
That I put on every day,
And pink is the colour of the roses
That I bought and forgot to pay.

Pink is the colour of my candyfloss
Yum, yum, yum,
And pink is the colour of tasty things,
Like bubblegum.

Pink is the colour of marshmallows,
Dipped in lots of cream,
And pink is the colour of sweeties,
A young child's dream.

Strawberry milk is a beautiful colour,
It is a baby pink.
But did you know pink is more popular than you think?

Becky Curtis-Harris (11)
Kempshott Junior School, Basingstoke

The Magic Box

(Based on 'Magic Box' by Kit Wright)

I will put in the box . . .
The swish of fur from a brown dog,
Fire from an exploding volcano,
The tip of a star reaching for the moon.

I will put in the box . . .
A snowman smiling at the white snow,
A sip of hope from a dying man,
A leaping whale through the wave of the bluest sea.

I will put in the box . . .
Three rainbows sitting in the sky,
The last teardrop of a lion,
And the first breath of a zebra being born.

Kelly Cummings (11)
Kempshott Junior School, Basingstoke

The Magic Box

(Based on 'Magic Box' by Kit Wright)

I will put in the box . . .
The swish of air running through my hair
Fire heating up the world like an inferno
The tip of the mountain piercing through the clouds.

I will put in the box . . .
A snowman standing in loneliness surrounded by a crowd
A sip of life running through our bodies
A leaping spark as an idea comes to life.

I will put in my box . . .
Three little children sitting all alone,
The last hope of peace finally succeeding,
And the first kiss of love to your father.

I will put in the box . . .
An eighth day and the only galaxy
A man at the bottom of the ocean
And a fish in his bed of sawdust.

My box is made from secrets
With love on top and hate in the corners
The hinges are made from wishes dying to happen.
I shall hide my box in my heart
And when I go it will travel from my heart to my children,
And will go on forever and evermore.

Laura Smith (11)
Kempshott Junior School, Basingstoke

The Magic Box

(Based on 'Magic Box' by Kit Wright)

I will put in the box . . .
The swish of night's velvet cloak
Fire from the centre of Sauron's eye
The tip of an ear that's heard a million words.

I will put in the box . . .
A snowman smiling as he melts into oblivion
A sip of the sweetest water form the invisible lakes of the moon
A leaping young deer scared of the night.

I will put in the box . . .
Three drops of water
The last is death
The first is birth.

I will put in the box . . .
A 25th hour of the day
An ancient Egyptian computer and a Canopic jar from the
                                        21st century.

My box is fashioned from fire and water, light and dark, Heaven
                                        and Hell.
The lid is made of gravity with death in the corners and hinges made
                                        of time.
I shall fly in my magic box,
Over cliffs and mountains into space, flying past planets and landing
                        on Jupiter, Mars and Saturn.

John Venner (11)
Kempshott Junior School, Basingstoke

The Magic Box

(Based on 'Magic Box' by Kit Wright)

I will put in the box . . .
The swish of a vicious vampire's cape,
Fire from a brilliant burning bonfire,
The tip of a pyramid touching a golden cloud.

I will put in the box . . .
A snowman melting in the moonlight,
A sip of the finest red wine,
A leaping lavender shooting out of the ground.

I will put in the box . . .
Three last barks from a dying dog,
The last leaves from a burning tree,
And the first ship built by the ancient Egyptians.

I will put in the box . . .
A twenty-fifth hour of the everlasting day,
An eighth day of the glorious week,
And a gigantic lion as big as a dinosaur.

My box is fashioned from a million icicles,
With famous remarkable gems.
Its hinges are made from the finest, most beautiful gold and silver.
I shall fly in my box on the clouds of the world,
Then when I land in Heaven, I shall rest for evermore!

Evienne Heynes (10)
Kempshott Junior School, Basingstoke

Is This Green?

Green tastes like the refreshing mouthwash I have every morning,
It feels like the calm lake waving at you,
Green is the smell of fresh grass flowing in the wind,
It is the sound of the laughter in the background,
Green looks like the grin of a four-leaf clover waiting to be picked.

Jazmine Johnson (11)
Kempshott Junior School, Basingstoke

The Magic Box

(Based on 'Magic Box' by Kit Wright)

I will put in the box . . .
The swish of the swaddling bandages our Lord Jesus Christ
                                                    was wrapped in.
Fire of Hell to burn for evermore tormenting the souls of the damned.
The tip of an ancient stalactite extinguishing a life like a wax candle
                                                    in a winter breeze.

I will put in the box . . .
A snowman made from God's oldest creation, a snowflake drifting
Down to sit on a newborn baby's palm.
A sip of life, which we take for granted, drunk by a man clad in red
With horns, surrounded by last sounds.
A leaping soul racing across the universe, hurrying to reach eternal
                                                    bliss.

I will put in the box . . .
Three newborn lambs, prancing around in a field carelessly, guarded
Closely by their mother.
The last breath of the last man, ever to tread the universe, shuddering,
Inching towards death.
The first smile of a newborn baby, sighting the world for the first time,
The world where his life will unfold.

I will put in the box . . .
A 398th day to the year, 7 weeks in the month, and 86 hours in a day.
A pterodactyl on an undersized novelty scooter,
A man in a pterodactyl nest being pecked to death.

My box is fashioned from sweat, blood and pain,
It has death on the lid and torture in the corners,
Its hinges are the bindings of the universe.

I shall gaze at my museum of objects inside my box
Have a gentle respite in an imaginary café
And then return to the hellish world, called my life.

Rhianne Rampton (11)
Kempshott Junior School, Basingstoke

The Magic Box

(Based on 'Magic Box' by Kit Wright)

I will put in my box . . .
The swish of a bullet piercing the night air
Fire from the barrel of a tank
The tip of bombs falling on Germany.

I will put in my box . . .
A snowman melting as the allied troops advance
A sip of the dying water in a canister
A leaping man jumping for life.

I will put in my box . . .
One last light in a world full of darkness.
Three countries that have united
A tiny drop of hope in a world full of mystery.

I will put in my box . . .
The last man trying to rule the world
And the first smile on a child's face.

I will put in my box . . .
A new world and a new life
Every human never fighting with no one dying.

My box is made of love and peace
The lock is England, America and Russia.
The corners are the four corners of the Earth.
I shall lock all these memories away
And forget about it for all time.

Alistair Miller (11)
Kempshott Junior School, Basingstoke

The Magic Box

(Based on 'Magic Box' by Kit Wright)

I will put in the box . . .
The swish of an unicorn sweeping its territory with its magic touch.
Fire from the depth of your heart warning you with each beat
of survival.
The tip of the mountain watching the world turn like time
never-ending.

I will put in the box . . .
A snowman with a broken heart
A sip of peace covering the Earth with its velvet blanket.
A leaping spark of faith spreading within your heart.

I will put in the box . . .
Three worlds yet to be born into the galaxy's arms.
The last dream drifting through your mind
And the first wish made by a lonely child waiting for a family.

I will put in the box . . .
An eighth day of the week and a dull night sky.
A book with no words
And a universe with no planets.

My box is styled with peace, joy and hope
With love on the lid and secrets in the corners.
Its hinges are made from the centre of the mystical stars.

I shall live in my box, in the depth of my heart for years to come,
Then ride to Heaven with my emotions locked up.

Pooja Rabheru (11)
Kempshott Junior School, Basingstoke

The Magic Box

(Based on 'Magic Box' by Kit Wright)

I will put in my box . . .
The swish of death's hand as it claims lost souls
Fire from the depths of Hell
The tip of a blue flame consuming the world.

I will put in the box . . .
A snowman with a forgotten smile
A sip of the life blood from the earth
A leaping piece of a captured star.

I will put in the box . . .
Three bottles of distilled pain
The last breath of a dying child
And the first scream of a suffering man.

I will put in the box . . .
An eighth day and a sleepless night
A dead fly in a frantic world
A sad ornament being blown apart.

My box is made from the torment of the old world encrusted with
Steel and flame with torture lining it,
Its hinges are the suffering of others.
I shall lock my box with hope and keep it in the darkest depths
Of my heart.

Terry Sibley (10)
Kempshott Junior School, Basingstoke

The Magic Box

(Based on 'Magic Box' by Kit Wright)

I will put in the box . . .
The swish from the feather of a soaring eagle in the everlasting sky,
Fire from a single campfire slowly dying in the golden desert,
The tip of a needle, as a lonely mum sews her lost son a shirt.

I will put in the box . . .
A snowman standing steady in the drifting snow,
A sip of warm tea on a cold winter's day,
A leaping mountain climber jumping across the frozen peaks.

I will put in the box . . .
Three little kittens who have lost their mum to a savage dog,
The last sight of everyone's terror,
And the first sight of love.

I will put in the box . . .
A fifth friend that helps and cares,
A sad elephant with a beak,
And a confused eagle with a trunk.

My box is created with golds and silvers
With exquisite emeralds and radiant rubies.
It has dragon talons as hinges.
I shall spend my life in the bewitching box
And see the items in my box.
Then come out and hand it to my adoring grandson
So he can be happy also.

Toby Foley (11)
Kempshott Junior School, Basingstoke

The Magic Box

(Based on 'Magic Box' by Kit Wright)

I will put in the box . . .
The swish of the murderous river running down a sacred hill.
Fire from evil's lair defeating good, praising bad.
The tip of a pen writing out the world's story.

I will put in the box . . .
A snowman's melting emotions restoring them once again.
A sip of life pouring into a baby's first breath.
A leaping jump of love filling the world with happiness.

I will put in the box . . .
Three reckless nights surviving throughout hidden worlds,
The last broken heart searching for love once more.
The first dream of the ocean riding through salty seas.

I will put in the box . . .
A second heart in case one breaks,
A person with a rich book cover,
And a book with human skin.

My box is dressed from royal riches with hearts on the lid
And whispers in the corner.
Its hinges are the swooping wings of a butterfly.
I shall swim in my box in a forever lasting ocean,
Then stop in the velvet night sky.
The colour of dreams.

Amber Connolly (11)
Kempshott Junior School, Basingstoke

The Magic Box

(Based on 'Magic Box' by Kit Wright)

I will put in the box . . .
The swish of a dolphin's fin, riding over the horizon,
Fire trailing behind the moon as it tours the galaxy,
The tip of a unicorn's horn brushing peace over the world for
all eternity.

I will put in the box . . .
A snowman waiting, watching for the flicker of a shooting star
To pass and make his dreams come true.
A sip from the depths of the turquoise ocean,
A leaping pen jubilantly waiting to write a carpet of words
over the world.

I will put in the box . . .
Three unspoken whispers waiting to be unravelled.
The last drop of water wasted by humanity
And the first laugh of the waves.

I will put in the box . . .
An eighth day of the week
A beach with no waves
And a world with no night.

My box is wooden with welded brass swirls
With secrets on the lid and wishes on the corners,
Its hinges are sparkles of diamonds.
I shall make a wish on each corner
To make all dreams come true
Then come ashore on a sandy beach
Where the wish will be fulfilled.

Sian Swyny (11)
Kempshott Junior School, Basingstoke

What Is Blue?

Blue smells like a pebbly beach's salty air,
It smells like mild berries freshly picked for a funfair.
Even a sweet ripple wafting to your red nose so bare.

Blue looks like the white frothed sea on a calm summer's day
It looks like delicious blueberries hanging on a spiny bush facing
every way.
Even a dangling bluebell on a atom-bed it lay.

Blue tastes like the bitter salty sea,
It tastes like a mouth watering berry to complete a kingdom,
Without what would it be?
Even sweet nectar for a passing bumblebee.

Blue feels like the gentle sea soothing your rough foot,
The blueberry feels rough, but delicate for you to eat,
Even soft fragile petals found by a secret creek.

Blue is a sea drifting around,
It's like a blue moon spinning around,
Even a blue ballerina skirt dancing and swishing around.

That is what blue is!

Gabriella Clarke (11)
Kempshott Junior School, Basingstoke

What Is Green?

Green is the sign of evil lurking in the midnight sky,
Green is the colour of a rattlesnake, hissing away in the itchy grass.

Green is the smell of chillies lying hot between the kebab fillings.
Hear the green grasshoppers jumping from each strand of grass.

Watch an apple tree growing steadily in the spring weather.
Watch people staring at you with their green pupils.

See Manor Field playing happily in their green uniform.
Hear the natural environment seeking their prey.

So now you know green is more popular than you think.

Richard Oliver (11)
Kempshott Junior School, Basingstoke

What Is White?

White tastes of vanilla ice cream melting in my mouth
White looks like the snow falling in the south.

White feels like ice-cold snow in my hand
White looks like the fluffy clouds floating around
In the snow filled sky.

White sounds like snow splatting against the window.
I am looking out at the moment with tired eyes.
White is the colour which makes you sit near a fire.

White smells like the frothy milk of a newly poured cappuccino.
White is the colour of the paper I am writing on.

White tastes of luscious cat's milk,
White looks like a wedding dress made of fine silk.
So to all those people that don't think white is a colour,
They are wrong!

Sam Nightingale (11)
Kempshott Junior School, Basingstoke

Colour Poem

Red, yellow, blue or green,
Which one shall I pick?

Yellow, yellow that's the one,
Let's have a look.
Yellow is the colour that is butter, hiding my potato,
And summer's simple dancing days passing through my eyes.
A shrivelled up old person, with nothing much to say.
Their life filled with golden sheaves of happiness and surely
some of joy.
Have you ever smelled the signs that spring has come?
Daffodils, daisies and other things.
Now is the time to end this poem but from Andrew Allen,
Goodbye is for now.

Andrew Allen (11)
Kempshott Junior School, Basingstoke

What Is Pink?

Pink is sweet sugary candyfloss.
Right next to the circular ring toss.
Pink is a new expensive dress,
With a beautiful green cress.
Pink is like a Power Ranger in combat
Next to a black tabby cat.
Pink is a sunsetting on a luscious day.
It's also melting milkshake making its way.
Pink is the colour of Miss Hat's car,
Which can't travel very far.
I'm using Chole's pink pencil at this moment in time.
Pink is the colour to prevent crime.
Pink is a flamingo standing on one leg,
While laying a spotty pink egg.

Ryan Case (11)
Kempshott Junior School, Basingstoke

What Is Silver?

Silver is warm milk,
And as soft as silk.

The shining moon reflects off the pond like sun off a mirror,
Rebounding the shimmery glimmer.

Silver sounds like a magical flute,
And looks like a silver buckled boot.

Silver is a shining sword,
Or the sails in a boat that's moored.

Silver is crystals in a cave.
Silver is diamonds on a ring,
Shining, shimmering.

Andrew Spencer (11)
Kempshott Junior School, Basingstoke

What Is Blue?

Blue is a cool icy water, as fresh as a loaded mortar.
Blue is a tropical water in the Caribbean,
Waiting to be swum in by tourists.
Blue is the amazing Arsenal away kit, shining and light.
Blue is the colour of a Ferrari Enzo,
Glistening its neon lights in the wind.
Blue is the colour of a beautiful night,
Glimmering at midnight.
Blue is the colour of a glowing light sabre,
Like Darth Vader doing you no favour.
Blue is the colour of Italy's home kit,
Showing off a bit!

Now you know blue is the *b-e-e-e-st* colour!

Jamie Kelly (11)
Kempshott Junior School, Basingstoke

What Is Cream?

Cream is the colour of vanilla ice cream,
Cream is the colour of a really good dream,
Cream is the colour of the moon glaring down,
Cream is the colour of a silky dressing gown.

Cream is the colour of smooth beach shells,
Cream is the colour of small, gentle bells,
Cream is the colour of a soft suede belt,
Cream is the smell of chocolate about to melt.

Cream is the colour of a freshly laid egg,
Cream is the colour of a smooth, wooden peg,
Cream is the colour of the cake I'm slicing,
Cream is the colour of butter icing.

Camilla Johnson (11)
Kempshott Junior School, Basingstoke

What Is Pink?

Candyfloss is pink!
Cuddling tiny candy crystals,
It is a woman with a new necklace.

A sunset is pink.
It looks like blended colours,
In a painting.

Marshmallows are pink!
They melt in your mouth,
It is a piece of metal being smouldered in a fire.

True love is pink!
It blossoms in the moonlight as,
You have your first kiss.

But this is what pink means to me!
It feels like happiness and joy,
It smells like sweet pollen wafting around you,
It looks like glowing grace and beauty,
Its touch is comforting and soft,
Its taste is sensational.

But what do you think of pink?

Hannah Owens (11)
Kempshott Junior School, Basingstoke

What Is Pink?

Pink is . . .
. . . the tangy, bitter taste of a ripened pink grapefruit,
. . . the pink Mercedes going a-toot-toot-toot.

. . . Luscious prawns burning on a fire,
. . . they will fill your heart's desire.

. . . Bath bombs with an essence like Heaven,
. . . the sweet candyfloss you get from Devon.

. . . Flamingos standing on one leg,
. . . a baby whose name is Meg.

Georgina Smith (11)
Kempshott Junior School, Basingstoke

What Is Brown?

What is brown?
Brown is bugs crawling over crisp wood piles.
Brown is also mud lying on the ground,
Like a boy sleeping on the streets.
Lastly, brown is the hair on your very own head,
Waiting to get cut at the hairdressers.

What is brown?
Brown smells like jealousy boiling in your mind.
Brown is also chocolate running down your throat slowly.
Lastly, brown is a mole popping up for light from underground.

What is brown?
Brown tastes like poison infecting your blood.
Brown is also a rabbit nibbling a carrot uncontrollably.
Lastly, brown is the colour of war and pain.

Chris Smith (11)
Kempshott Junior School, Basingstoke

Blue

Blue is a whale jumping through the air
Blue is a person dyeing their hair.

Blue is the ocean washing my feet
Blue is Dory being shark's meat.

Blue is an octopus spreading its ink
Blue is the thoughts that I think.

Blue is paint washing the walls
Blue is a pen making scribbles.

Blue is a car zooming down the road
Blue is a lunch trolley carrying a small load.

Jack Hallinan (11)
Kempshott Junior School, Basingstoke

What Green Could Be

Green could be the colour of the paper
I am writing on.
Green could be the colour of the fearsome dragons
In people's dreams.
Green could be the main colour of a dancing rainbow
In the sky.
Green could be the colour of the dye in someone's hair.
Green could be the colour of the paint on the end of
Your brush.
Green could be the colour of a camouflaged snake smiling.
Green could be the colour of some people's eyes
Blinking at the sun.
Green could be the colour of trees and plants with grass
Climbing around and around again.

So what do you think green could be in your mind?

Kimberley Parrott (11)
Kempshott Junior School, Basingstoke

Purple

Purple is the colour of a box of brand new scrunchies.

Purple feels warm, fuzzy and soft like a fresh duvet.

Purple is the colour of a soft ice cream coated in crispy
purple Smarties.

Purple is the colour of a fluffy cloud, shimmering at sunset.

A parrot has a purple streak running down its tail, which makes
him want to sing through the rainforest.

Purple is the colour of beautiful sweet smelling lavender.

Deanna Moss (11)
Kempshott Junior School, Basingstoke

Springful

I am a speedy, cheerful maniac
A fearful kid who is wonderful
I'm joyful whilst I'm speeding down the track
My style is sporty 'n' colourful
I'm terrified whilst running round the red course,
And you can't look absolutely beautiful,
I eat a lot of vegetables which helps,
I produce lots of power, they say I'm fruitful.

My netball skills are tactful so that is brill,
I am in the netball team, I'm very grateful.
Everyone works together even though we are quite playful.
We try to concentrate - careful!
Sometimes we're losing, so we work together - cheerful!
My legs are long and this is making me springful.

I can jump like a kangaroo and leap like a deer
But that's because I'm tall and slim - powerful!
I love to jump long distances and leap like a hare
But sometimes I slip and fall. But I don't care.

That is the end of my sport's career,
Hope you liked it.

Ellie Cameron (9)
Kingswood Primary School, Tadworth

Playful

I was lined up for the race, hopeful,
Then the whistle blew and I got a steady pace.
Five wonderful minutes later I was wonderful in front.
I ran very careful
And then there was five helpful steps and success.
I finished the race first.
I was thankful.

Greg Fowler (10)
Kingswood Primary School, Tadworth

Indescribable

There's nothing better than sport,
The fun is indescribable,
You're going to like it,
You'll be sure to stay stable!
Go and try it, have a go,
Sit there and look miserable?
That's really not possible!

Michael Newman (10)
Kingswood Primary School, Tadworth

Possible

I'm an all-round super genius,
Everything for me is possible,
I can easily make you laugh,
Even though I'm so miserable.

I have a go at everything
If I am rather suitable.
I try hard at anything I do,
Because nothing is impossible.

Tony Graham (10)
Kingswood Primary School, Tadworth

Graceful

I am a fab great flexible gymnast
My dazzling rhythm is really graceful,
They say I look a natural gymnastic,
My splits are extremely painful,
My cartwheels may make people laugh sometimes,
But I'm extraordinary and wonderful,
I am a fab great flexible gymnast,
My dazzling rhythm is really graceful.

Danni Gibbs (9)
Kingswood Primary School, Tadworth

Artful

I am playful
I am joyful
I hate the meaning of dreadful
I never give up
So I am hopeful.
I describe it as artful
I like the meaning of colourful
My pictures are wonderful
If people help me . . .
I'll be very thankful
I'm also very careful
I'm sometimes very useful
I sometimes can become harmful
When bad, I'm shameful,
When good, I'm grateful.

Catriona Barber (10)
Kingswood Primary School, Tadworth

Wonderful

I am a gymnastic maniac
I think I am quite wonderful
When I am turning somersaults
My friends say I am dreadful
I just overlook their words
Because I am so forgetful.
I don't mind hanging upside-down
Because I am not fearful.
A cosmopolitan champion,
I am very hopeful
My friend's leotards are dull
Whilst mine is colourful.
I am a gymnastic maniac
I think I am quite wonderful.

Gemma East (10)
Kingswood Primary School, Tadworth

Helpful

I am a helpful maniac.
My style is cool and *helpful*.
My lyrics make her laugh sometimes,
As well as being *playful*.

I'll send him up, and up the wall,
I'll make him act *pitiful*.
Each word is flaming, and can't be held
I suppose he'd say I'm *lethal*.
Just to protect my people
When enemies try and put me down,
I can't see them, they're the wrong way round.
I love rhythms and my beats
I think they're very *joyful*.
The people I care for and love too,
They think my rhymes are *successful*.
I am a helpful manic, and that's all I have to say.

Jodie Fahey (10)
Kingswood Primary School, Tadworth

Playful

I am a total scouby maniac,
Playful, hopeful and plentiful.
My scoubies make people gasp and stare,
As well as being colourful.
I make you act weird and wild,
I am very, very wonderful.
If I was really bored and sad,
I wouldn't be cool and fruitful.
My hands are really quick and fast,
While I am being cheerful.
My friends think I am brilliant,
I just think scoubies are delightful.

Charlene Lok (9)
Kingswood Primary School, Tadworth

Wonderful

Some people call me dreadful
But I'm rather beautiful
I can be really peaceful
I want to be mega playful
But some people are not as cheerful
I think I'm being forgetful
Because I forget to water the plants
I like to dress colourfully
I'm also really fearful
I want to be helpful
And I'm extra careful
I always try to be hopeful
As well as being wonderful.

Oliver Hazel (10)
Kingswood Primary School, Tadworth

Playful

I am a Game Cube maniac.
I like to be so playful.
But when it comes to racing
I am absolutely wonderful.
When it comes to fighting,
I am like a Viking.
When I'm on my own, I am pitiful.
But when a friend comes, I'm indestructible,
And all my friends say I'm successful.
Even though I'm hogwash at flying,
It's still like a world of gaming.
And in conclusion I am wonderful.

Harry Naef (10)
Kingswood Primary School, Tadworth

Tearful

If I was made a first buddy
I would be so cheerful
I would dance around the house,
With the buddy that made me tearful.
I would cry a waterful of tears,
But these tears are beautiful.
So now I know the thing that makes me happy,
Is a buddy who makes me joyful.

Lauren Simmons (10)
Kingswood Primary School, Tadworth

Colourful

I painted a speckly glittery picture
Which is pretty colourful
My picture shone so beautiful
People came to see the wonderful picture
They wanted to buy the picture so cheerful
To put on their wall
They said it was the best picture
They had ever had, so wonderful.

Stephanie Clarke (10)
Kingswood Primary School, Tadworth

Artful

My painted pictures are wonderful,
They develop into something artful,
They are so bright and colourful,
My photos are powerful,
My frames are beautiful,
My colours are very hopeful,
I am the coolest artist. Thanks
With the ideas in my head; useful.

Ella Beagley (10)
Kingswood Primary School, Tadworth

Skilful

In netball I am careful
I'm also very skilful
In a game I am hopeful
In a match I am useful
In a tournament I'm beautiful
Super Sian can win a goal!
I try my hardest to win!

Sian Wells (9)
Kingswood Primary School, Tadworth

Space

I am a little tiger
I decided to go to space
I met a group of aliens
Who took me to their base.

I had a little mission
There to defeat the evil race.

I drove a UFO to Planet Manamace,
I started to lose control over it
And flew into the king's face!

The king of the evil aliens
He was really in a rage,
He looked like an alien bird called
A 'Swollen Cockledage'.

I had the evil aliens all chasing after me.
This was a serious case.
But for them it was a serious chase.

I jumped off a cliff but held onto the edge of it,
With the wind as cold as ice.
All the evil aliens jumped after me,
But didn't see me hanging,
And so the story ends, as I was said to be . . .
    The Ace of Space!

Adrian Hobbs (8)
Lytchett Matravers Primary School, Poole

Sunnybun's Adventures

In England there was a bunny,
It's name was Sunnybun,
She smelt a bit like honey
It was rather funny.

She hopped along a grassy field,
With little circles of daisies.
Inside were buttercups in the shape of a shield,
On this grassy field.

Then she hopped onto a sandy beach,
Where the sun shone like gold.
Sunny sun, funny fun,
She hopped in the sea, and shivered, because of the cold.

Then *'boom, clang'* a football bounced,
An Arsenal player appeared!
It was Henry,
When he saw Sunnybun, he chucked her in the sea!

Samantha Hacklett (8)
Lytchett Matravers Primary School, Poole

Football

Once I went to a football match and waved my hands about like mad.
I nearly got earache,
There were so many people shouting.
Suddenly a football came down from the sky,
And landed on my heel.
I got such a surprise.
I threw it back on the football pitch
And then one of the football players shouted back,
'Thank you.'

Shannon Johnson (8)
Lytchett Matravers Primary School, Poole

Pet's Pets

I have a pet rabbit called Wonky.
I have two goldfish, one called Goldie and one is called Glittery.
I have a dog called Barcey,
He chases my rabbit around the house.
I love my pets a lot.
My rabbit is cute,
My rabbit is pretty and all of the others are too.
I feed them every day.
My dog chases my dad's slipper.
My fish swim in the fish tank all around.
My fish swim around the shells in the fish tank.
My rabbit is grey.
My fish are orange.
My dog is brown.
All my pets are princesses.

Chelsea Carter (8)
Lytchett Matravers Primary School, Poole

Football!

My team is the best
Our goalie called Charlie is amazing.
He hasn't let a goal in.
Our defender is called Max.
He is good at tackling people.
Our other defender called Jack has a big kick.
Our midfielder called Todd is good at scoring headers,
Our other midfielder called Ryan is good at free-kicks,
Our other midfielder called Harry is good at throw-ins.
Our forward called Sam is good at setting goals up for
Our other forward called Nathaniel,
Who is good at scoring and that is that.

Nathaniel Long (8)
Lytchett Matravers Primary School, Poole

Pets

The cute cats
And the vicious rats
Are friends.

The big tarantula
And the lion
Are not friends.

The amazing dogs
And the hedgehogs
Are friends.

The pig is not friends
With the frog
In the bog.

The black bat
And rat called Pat
Are best friends.

Eleanor Walls (7)
Lytchett Matravers Primary School, Poole

Pets

I have a rabbit called Kelly
She is furry and her collar is white and grey.
I have two cats and one of them is tabby.
I used to have two guinea pigs
One was called Tigger,
The other was called Winnie.
My friend has a dog called Barney.
He is a bulldog and is white and brown.
He has a long tongue.

Erin Hopper (7)
Lytchett Matravers Primary School, Poole

The Playground

There is a huge playground
After lessons me and my friends go to the sweet shop.
We have candy, mints, bubblegum, any flavours.
Me and my friend Summer go to the skate park.
We've eaten our sweets already.
We skate side to side.
We go to the bay hut and get a hotdog.
When we've finished them,
We go to the sweet shop.
We have the Mini Tones.
They pipped and popped.
The sherbet was sour.
It tickled and sizzled.
We went back to the skate park.
We skated, we stopped,
We walked to my house
And slept.

Amy Barr (8)
Lytchett Matravers Primary School, Poole

Seasons

There are four seasons in a year,
Spring, summer, autumn, winter.

In spring, the flowers start blooming
And the trees start budding.

In summer all the baby animals are born
And the sun starts shining.

In autumn the leaves turn brown and the wind
Gives out angry growls.

In winter it is chilly and it begins to snow.

Hollie Bryant (8)
Lytchett Matravers Primary School, Poole

Pets

My kittens eat rabbit and lamb and tuna and chicken.
My fish eats fish food that is in flakes.
My dog eats tinned food.
My budgies eat bird food that is seeds.
My dog has five balls.
My kittens have one red ball, two fishing rods,
one mouse that they take in the house.
My fish has no toys but he is greedy.
My budgies have one bird toy and two mirrors.
My dog sleeps in a huge green bed.
My kittens sleep in a red bed with cats asleep on it.
My fish sleeps in his bowl.
My budgies sleep in their cage.
My dog is called Tuppy,
but sometimes we call her Puppy.
My kittens are called Jasper and Bex.

Lucy Farrant (8)
Lytchett Matravers Primary School, Poole

The Policeman Kennings

Crime catcher
Door detacher
Busy worker
Silent lurker
Car chaser
Crime facer
Hand cuffer
Getting rougher
Letter writer
Crime fighter.

Ben Sharman (9)
Lytchett Matravers Primary School, Poole

Football

We are in second place
We have an amazing captain called Patrick Vieira.
We have a brilliant goalkeeper called Lehmann
We have Thierry Henry
He is the best forward
Our best midfielder is Robert Pires
The best and coolest defender is Ashley Cole
Robin van Persie is one of the best forwards too.

Lucas Jones (8)
Lytchett Matravers Primary School, Poole

Gerrard

G arcia is his brilliant partner
E nemy Roy Keane gets in his way
R onaldinho is his death demon
R unning like a cheetah
A nxioius to be England captain
R otten Man U make him go crazy
D ynamite Gerrard.

Sidney Longworth (9)
Lytchett Matravers Primary School, Poole

Animals

Skunks smell of poo.
Monkeys are bony and skinny.
Elephants smell and are very big.
Baboons are fluffy.
Dolphins are smooth.
Rabbits are very cuddly.

Ben Short (7)
Lytchett Matravers Primary School, Poole

Doctor Who

Alien chaser
Time racer
World saver
Big favour
Time lord
No sword
TARDIS keeper
Time leaper
TV star
No car
Time folder
Rose holder
Science lover
Undercover
Quick thinker
Non drinker
Big clue
Doctor Who!

Dhiren Leal (9)
Lytchett Matravers Primary School, Poole

Pets

I have a dog called Trixie
She chews my mother's plant
My mother goes mad
My mother smacks her
Trixie goes off crying in her bed
And sulks for the rest of the night
So she will get another smack
She will go off crying in her bed for the day.
She will get bored
So I will have to take her for a walk.

Charlie Dennett (8)
Lytchett Matravers Primary School, Poole

Cat Kennings

Door scratcher
Mouse snatcher
Fish eater
Rat beater
Bug reaper
Sofa keeper
Fence walker
Hamster stalker
Floor creeper
Mouse reaper
Shoe ripper
Person tripper
Death bringer
Ball flinger.

George Wood (9)
Lytchett Matravers Primary School, Poole

Food

When I was a year old I ate all of the chocolates
Off the Christmas tree.
When I was two I slobbered over the jelly, and it went stale.
My mum was fed up so she kept me out of the kitchen.

But when I was six I ate my mum's chocolate
Because I got in the kitchen.

When I was twenty-one I was brilliant,
When I was twenty-two I popped a sausage.
When I was twenty-three I was a great cook.

But . . .

When I was forty I was the best cook in the world.
Bang! I popped the sausage
Again . . .

James Belchamber (8)
Lytchett Matravers Primary School, Poole

Animals

A nimals are smelly
B ugs are dirty
C ars are pretty
D ogs are handsome
E lephants are rough
F ish are smooth
G iraffes are tall
H orses are fast
I guanas are lizards
J aguars are black
K angaroos are bouncy
L ions are scary
M ice are small
N ewts are slippery
O ctopuses have eight arms
P enguins waddle
Q is a secret
R hinos are rough
S nakes are long
T arantulas are deadly
U nicorns are magic
V elociraptors were dinosaurs
W orms are tiny
X is another secret
Y aks are like us
Z ebras have huge stripes.

Callum Whiteford (7)
Lytchett Matravers Primary School, Poole

Sarah

S hiny blonde hair
A lways looking out for her friends
R eally happy when eating sweets
A nd lovely dinners cooked by her mum
H appy and smiling having a great time.

Sarah Ayley (9)
Lytchett Matravers Primary School, Poole

Seasons

The winter is cold and draughts come through the door.
Outside it is snowing.

The winter is cold
The summer is hot
The spring is colourful
The autumn is dull.

The summer is hot and sunny
Everyone goes down to the stream.

The winter is cold
The summer is hot
The spring is colourful
The autumn is dull.

The spring is colourful with flowers
And birds singing.

The winter is cold
The summer is hot
The spring is colourful
The autumn is dull.

The autumn is dull
With brown crispy leaves
You hear the leaves crunch
When you step on them.

And that is all the seasons.

Holly Miles (8)
Lytchett Matravers Primary School, Poole

Lady From Poole

There was a young lady from Poole
Who went every day to school
Because it was far
She travelled by car
And was always late as a rule.

Lauren Graham (8)
Lytchett Matravers Primary School, Poole

The Owl

Night-time soarer
Daytime snorer
Mouse chaser
Sky racer
High rider
Low glider
Slow swooper
Good looper
Meat taker
Nest maker
Eyes bright
Good sight
Small brain
Hates rain.

Annabel Mulholland (9)
Lytchett Matravers Primary School, Poole

Guess What?

Meat eater
Cat beater
Ball chaser
Human racer
Good hider
Rubbish rider
Bone finder
Meat grinder
Deep lover
Undercover
Happy player
Ground layer.

Becky Downs (9)
Lytchett Matravers Primary School, Poole

Puppy

Bone snatcher
Stick catcher

Cat chaser
Fast pacer

Happy player
Ground layer

Deep sleeper
Toy keeper

Ball teaser
Toy seizer

Person chaser
Even pacer.

Matt Holland (9)
Lytchett Matravers Primary School, Poole

Guess Who?

Chelsea winger
Goal bringer
Brilliant crosser
Glory tosser
Chance taker
Goal maker
Ball flicker
Goalie tricker
Posh dresser
Opposition messer
Team forgiver
Goal trigger.

Xander Ettling (9)
Lytchett Matravers Primary School, Poole

Guess Who?

Crowd delighter
Letter writer
Dog lover
Brilliant mother
Throne sitter
Crown glitter
Posh dresser
Christian blesser
Big house
No woodlouse.

The Queen.

Charlotte Miles (9)
Lytchett Matravers Primary School, Poole

The Environment Around Us

The long grass is waving in the blowy wind
Shadows are underneath the trees and bushes
The sun is blazing high in the sky
Above the trees and bushes.
The birds are chirping from the trees and bushes.

Animals like the environment and the habitats around us.

Daniel Lake (8)
Lytchett Matravers Primary School, Poole

Summer

S ea shimmering in the bright light
U mbrellas keeping people in the cool shade
M ums are watching children play with their colourful balls
M en are giving delicious freezing ice cream out
E xcited children swimming in the cold sea
R unning dog on the beach by the rocks.

Megan Single (8)
Lytchett Matravers Primary School, Poole

My Hamster

Deep starer
Fur wearer
Peanut eater
Wheel runner
Bed maker
Cage explorer
Food storer
Good listener
Big eater.

Charlotte Rubenstein (9)
Lytchett Matravers Primary School, Poole

Freaky Monster

Train lover
Cabbage hater
Big brother
Horrid traitor
Ant squasher
Bean eater
Car washer
Game cheater!

George Woods (9)
Lytchett Matravers Primary School, Poole

Animals

A nts acting to climb up slippery rocks.
N asty monkeys stealing bananas
I nsects running around on the hard rocks
M ammals staying outside in the freezing wild
A nimals eating up their prey
L ions licking themselves to stay clean
S nakes slithering in the shady grass.

Christopher Pillinger (9)
Lytchett Matravers Primary School, Poole

Guess Who?

Wimbledon winner
Tennis spinner.

Smash mayor
Tennis player.

Good smacker
Ball hacker.

Racquet hitter
Frying fritter.

Twin sister
Girl's mister.

Serena Williams.

Jodie Ellis (8)
Lytchett Matravers Primary School, Poole

Spring

Baby lambs
Just born.

Mowing lawn
Cutting corn.

Sky blue
Sea too.

Children skipping
Pond dipping.

At school
Kicking balls.

Spring's here
At last!

Megan Ackrell (8)
Lytchett Matravers Primary School, Poole

Dog

Ball chaser
Cat facer

Tongue loller
Tight collar

People lover
Undercover

Doorbell seeker
Floor sneaker

Fierce snarler
Gone *la-la*

Door scratcher
Mat catcher.

Dog!

Patricia Baldwin (9)
Lytchett Matravers Primary School, Poole

Spring

Lambs born
On lawn

Flowers grow
Men mow

Bunnies hopping
Never stopping

Spring breeze
In trees.

Libby Lamb (8)
Lytchett Matravers Primary School, Poole

Winter

W ailing winds groaning and moaning bending trees

I cicles dripping freezing water every day

N orth Pole temperature, wrap up warm

T rees covered in sparkly, glittery frost all day round

E veryone building snowmen in the cold winter snow

R eady for exciting presents on happy Christmas Day.

William Fowler (9)
Lytchett Matravers Primary School, Poole

Spring

S preading flowers all over fields

P ick the beautiful flowers one by one

R abbits chumping all the grass

I n the spring flowers bloom red, white and blue

N ewborn chicks hatching in the barn

G ood spring has arrived.

Emily Chamberlain (9)
Lytchett Matravers Primary School, Poole

Winter

W inds are blowing wild all around

I ce is everywhere on the ground

N uts are hanging on the tinkling tree

T ea and hot chocolate are being sipped carefully

E xcited people waiting for Christmas

R ain is coming again for spring.

Lauren Lloyd-Evans (8)
Lytchett Matravers Primary School, Poole

The Pig That Flew To The Moon

George the pig flew to the moon
On a silver spoon.

He ate a lot of cheese
And fell down on his knees.

When he was there, he had such fun
Eating cheese and hot cross buns.

On Monday he went to the sun
And shot Superman with a gun.

On Tuesday he came back extremely pink
And took a bath in Kryptonite's sink.

On Wednesday he was very lazy
And went out with a pig called Daisy.

On Thursday he went to Mars with a bad smell,
And came back with a long story to tell.

Megan Horlock (9)
Lytchett Matravers Primary School, Poole

Noises

A dog barks, *woof, woof!*
A cat miaows, *miaow, miaow!*
We talk, *chat chat!*
A parrot squawks, *squawk, squawk!*
A horse neighs, *neigh, neigh!*
A mouse squeaks, *squeak, squeak!*

These are the noises
You will hear here and there
There and here
They are the noises everywhere.

Jade Rumens (8)
Lytchett Matravers Primary School, Poole

Homer Simpson

Beer boozer
Fat loser
Bad worker
Sneaky lurker
Nice cruiser
Maggie loser
Bad driver
Smelly skiver
Snoring snoozer
Duff oozer
Burns's worker
Girl flirter
Marge's lover
Rich brother.

James Duncan (8)
Lytchett Matravers Primary School, Poole

Cat

Mouse chaser
Good racer
Deep sleeper
Boundary keeper
Sofa ripper
Tail whipper
Loud howler
Dog scowler
Eye flicker
Body licker.

Natalie Taylor (9)
Lytchett Matravers Primary School, Poole

Guess Who?

Fast leaper
No keeper

Good runner
No drummer

Olympic winner
Medal bringer

Good taker
No breaker

Fast chaser
Excellent racer

No loser
Race chooser.

Lauren Churchill (9)
Lytchett Matravers Primary School, Poole

Anakin Skywalker

Force barer
Jedi tearer
Evil maker
Darth Vader
Jedi traitor
Trade maker
Force breaker
Saber trader
Dark leader
Darth Vader.

Luca Infante (9)
Lytchett Matravers Primary School, Poole

Guess Who?

Ball kicker
Goal nicker
Penalty misser
Lady kisser
Boot cleaner
Post leaner
Left midfielder
Likes right midfielder
Good shooter
Good booter

David Beckham.

Daniel Amey (9)
Lytchett Matravers Primary School, Poole

Guess Who?

Grass stealer
Hair dealer
High hopper
Mole stopper
Hutch messer
Not dresser
Cat hater
Rabbit mater.

Naleisha Fisk (9)
Lytchett Matravers Primary School, Poole

Horse

H igh and tall as a tree
O n the hills eating away
R iding happily along the far trail
S ilk smooth so soft and shiny
E legant, pretty and full of love.

Jessica Taylor (8)
Lytchett Matravers Primary School, Poole

Monkey

Tree swinger
Banana bringer

Arm stretcher
Leaf fetcher

Flea eater
Card cheater

Noise maker
Good faker

Noisy sleeper
Cartoon weeper.

Gemma Cane (9)
Lytchett Matravers Primary School, Poole

Animals

A ll the animals hopping around
N aughty horses galloping up and down
I n the bushes you can see rabbits eating all the grass
M onkeys swinging from tree to tree
A nts are scuttling around over the dirty floor
L aughing hyenas echoing around the mountains
S nakes slithering around in a swirl.

Lara Pattison (8)
Lytchett Matravers Primary School, Poole

Monsters

There are bad monsters, there are mad monsters.
There are sneaky ones, there are streaky ones.
They have sharp teeth, they have spiky backs.
There are sad monsters, there are dad monsters.
There are monsters all around you.

Sam de Garis (8)
Lytchett Matravers Primary School, Poole

Winter

Wind is blowing wild and free
It twists around all the trees
Past the windows and through the town
Rain starts to fall and floods the ground.

Children slipping on the ice
Snow is falling from the sky
Families sitting by the fire
Outside the door there is a Christmas choir.

Lauren Collins (9)
Lytchett Matravers Primary School, Poole

Bigfoot

B ig feet, big foot
I   s Bigfoot real?
G iant footsteps are left
F eet so big they can crush your bones!
O ut in the wild, free to roam
O ut in the wild, hunting animals
T races of DNA left to study Bigfoot.

Lewis Blair (9)
Lytchett Matravers Primary School, Poole

Animals

A ntelopes dancing and prancing around,
N agging newts getting fat,
I   guanas crawling round,
M onkeys swinging from tree to tree
A ttacking alligators crunching up food
L eaping leopards running free
S low slugs creeping round.

Scott Horlock (9)
Lytchett Matravers Primary School, Poole

Pets

Dogs are playful when young,
But that means they have only just begun.
Cats are cute,
When they're on mute.
Guinea pigs are soft,
But there are rats in the loft.
Goldfish are gold,
But made for only water to hold.
Budgies make noise,
But they have no choice.
Hamsters only squeak,
Because they're weak.
Horses eat hay,
That's what makes them neigh.
Rabbits eat carrots,
Unlike parrots.

Millie Morgan (8)
Lytchett Matravers Primary School, Poole

Rainforest

Humid weather
Packed together

Human hunter
Tapir grunter

Vine swinger
Monkey flinger

Monkey howler
Plants flower

Trees taller
Trees smaller.

Oliver Matthews (9)
Lytchett Matravers Primary School, Poole

Homer Simpson

Fat loser
Lazy snoozer

Deep sleeper
Car beeper

Beef carver
Bart's father

Marge flirter
Blood squirter

Duff drinker
Bad thinker

Mad eater
Gamble cheater.

Oliver Levy (9)
Lytchett Matravers Primary School, Poole

The Dolphin

Wave rider
Sea glider

Ball whacker
Non slacker

Fast swimmer
Water skimmer

Non sleeper
Seaweed creeper

Sea dancer
Wave prancer

Beauty keeper
Shy peeper.

Rebecca Lewis (9)
Lytchett Matravers Primary School, Poole

Animals

A nts scurrying round and round
N ewts swimming through the water
 I guanas scuttling in the bush
M onkeys jumping in the trees
A ntelopes jumping up and down
L eopards stalking their prey
S nakes slithering on the ground.

Mitchell Taylor (9)
Lytchett Matravers Primary School, Poole

Our World

Think about all the things we've got
The treasures and the landscapes
Are all I have in the world.

All the buildings and houses,
The towns and cities
The insides of our bodies
The blood and veins are going round.
So all the things everywhere are important to me.

Gavin Brown (8)
Lytchett Matravers Primary School, Poole

Beano

I get the Beano weekly
With great glee
I like Dennis because he's a menace.
I like Minnie.
Minnie the Minx, she's always up to mischief.
Freddie Fear is so glum to have a witch as a mum.
Gnipper is Gnasher's son
Gnipper is quite fun.

Mark Scoble (7)
Lytchett Matravers Primary School, Poole

Footy Heroes

Chelsea Captain, John Terry
Has a beautiful wife called Cherry
Ronaldinho is the biggest star
He can kick the ball really far.

A good goalie is Van Der Sar
He has a wonderful car
My fave team is AFC Bournemouth
The best player has hurt his knee.

Cristiano Ronaldo has lots of tricks
He's superb at free-kicks
German legend Torsten Frings
Owns a lot of bling.

Bournemouth star Neil Moss
Has never liked the new boss
England legend Wayne Rooney
On a celebration, he does a moony.

Maradona is pretty big
He bumps into doors
At a restaurant
He begs for more.

Madrid Star Zinedine Zidane
When I'm watching him, I'm his biggest fan
The star Ryan Giggs
Likes to stroke pigs.

Jack Hawkins (9)
Lytchett Matravers Primary School, Poole

When I Eat Food

When I eat jelly it makes me want to watch the telly.
When I eat chips it makes me have salty lips.
When I eat pies I begin to say a lot of lies.
When I eat a bean it makes me feel very mean.

Ben de Garis (8)
Lytchett Matravers Primary School, Poole

Seasons

Spring is when new animals are born
And people love corn
New plants grow
Here comes the swooping crow.

Summer is when it's hot
And animals like it a lot
People swim in swimming pools
Also children don't go to schools.

Autumn is when the leaves fall
And trees are very tall
Red, orange, brown,
You can see them in the town.

Winter is when cosy fires are lit
And you get to sit
There are bare trees
As well as quivering knees.

Hannah Barr (10)
Lytchett Matravers Primary School, Poole

Michael Owen Kennings

Ball flicker
Goal kicker
Posh dresser
England messer
Bone breaker
Liverpool faker
Goal taker
Chelsea hater
House owner
Larry loner
Madrid stayer
England player
Injured hopper
Liverpool stopper.

Ryan Churchward (8)
Lytchett Matravers Primary School, Poole

The Seasons

Spring, summer, autumn and winter are the
Seasons of the year.

Spring is fresh and really bright
But it is still chilly in the night,
Newborn bunnies hop about,
But their mothers will still doubt,
If their babies will survive,
For the rest of their lives.

Summer is the best,
When you can have a rest,
We have holidays off school,
Now that is *cool!*

Autumn is when the leaves go brown,
And my mum begins to frown,
She lets me play in the woods sometime,
But my brother said, 'Don't be a long time.'

Winter is when it gets freezing cold,
And I got a new brother that is one week old.
Santa comes and gives us presents,
And my dad goes catching pheasants.

Jessica Lake (10)
Lytchett Matravers Primary School, Poole

Pets

Dogs are different to hogs
Because dogs chase mogs.
Dogs chase cats and cats chase rats.
They are mostly friends because they play fight
Sometimes they stay up all night.

At lunchtime they go out
To eat a bit of trout
They like the smell of meat,
But not stinky feet.

Georgia Collins (8)
Lytchett Matravers Primary School, Poole

The Sea

The sea is like a roller coaster
One minute it is still and calm
The next it's fast and rough
One minute it is hot
The next it's cold.

Listen carefully from the shore
To the different music playing
Soft and rippling like a flute or
Loud and crashing like cymbals
These are the sounds of the sea.

Surrounded by smooth golden sand
Brightly coloured sky and stony cliffs
Fish swimming happily in their homes
Excited and happy am I
All the reasons why I love the sea.

Tell me where your journey has taken you
What countries have you seen?
What secrets do you hide?
What mood are you in?
Please tell me my friend
The sea is a friend you must trust
The sea is like a roller coaster.

Jenny Matthews (10)
Lytchett Matravers Primary School, Poole

Mums

Mums are always there
Mums will always care
Mums will always love you
Mums will always send a dove above you
Mums will make you laugh
Mums will always say, 'Take a bath.'
Mums will look you in the eye
Mums can all tell when you're telling a lie.

Charli Webster (8)
Lytchett Matravers Primary School, Poole

I'll Be Waiting

When the sea crashes against the rock,
When the sky is blue,
When the sheepdog herds up the flock,
     I'll be waiting.

When the sun goes down,
When the stars are dancing,
When the cakes are crisp brown,
     I'll be waiting.

When the lambs are born,
When the river flows,
When you cut the corn,
     I'll be waiting.

When the horse starts to neigh,
When the sun is bright,
When the children play,
     I'll be waiting.

When you feel sad,
When the rosebuds open,
When the weather's bad,
     I'll be waiting.

When the fire's cold,
When spring turns to summer,
When the jelly's in its mould,
     I'll be waiting.

If you come back,
I promise,
No, when you come back, I promise,
     I'll still be waiting.

Rosemary Walls (10)
Lytchett Matravers Primary School, Poole

Peru

There once was a man from a strange place,
Who forgot to tie his shoelace,
He tripped on some ice,
Out of his head fell some lice,
It was a huge disgrace.

Then the brave and handsome headlice,
Decided to skate on some ice,
A knight followed their trace,
He was armed with a mace,
Because it was at a cheap price.

The strange man was from Peru,
He dreamed he was eating his shoe,
He woke with a fright,
In the middle of the night,
And found that his dream had come true.

The very same man from Peru,
Went for a ride in his canoe,
He died one stormy night,
Forgot to follow the light,
Now he's in Hell cleaning a loo.

His mum was as great as could be,
Until she fell out of a tree,
She cracked her head,
Now she's in bed,
Calling all day for her tea.

Her husband was called Lee,
He couldn't make good tea,
Lee had a goldfish,
It ate from a dish,
Now Lee's wife has coffee.

Tommy Holden (9)
Lytchett Matravers Primary School, Poole

Animals

Humphrey is a hamster,
He really is quite cute,
He can run around his wheel,
While I play the flute!

Crissie is a cat,
She enjoys her sleep,
I love her so, so much,
That's when she doesn't reek!

Dave is a dog,
He is very bold,
He's a super dooper dog,
That's why we named him Dave!

Lyn is a lizard,
Her scales are fairly rough,
She can be slick and scary,
And she can be tough!

I like these animals
That's why I wrote this poem,
Hope you will like this,
Maybe even Owen!

Maelle Swann (10)
Lytchett Matravers Primary School, Poole

Space

Space is fabulous
Better than sea
Better than tea.
Space is excellent
Better than being bold.
Space is marvellous
Better than bricks
Better than chicks.
Space is outstanding.

Rory Hover (8)
Lytchett Matravers Primary School, Poole

Buster

Buster is grey and white
He has the greatest eyesight.
He spots a rat
And all the blood goes splat.
Oh that darn cat!

He chases a string,
What a swifty thing.
Just like a blot of lightning,
His claws grasp at you, it's very frightening
Just like watching scary fighting.

He sits on your lap
Scratch and a slap.
His pointy claws
Oh and his jaws.
Always breaking kitty laws.

Buster is grey and white
He has the greatest eyesight.
He spots a rat.

And all the blood goes splat.
Oh that darn cat!

Caitlin McCarthy (9)
Lytchett Matravers Primary School, Poole

Sunset

In the red sky
Birds do fly
All going *tweet, tweet, tweet,*
And under their wings we do meet
Watching the sun go down
With a smile on our face, not a frown
The sun has set
And we have met
But it's time to go home now.

Eliza Atkinson (8)
Lytchett Matravers Primary School, Poole

Mary's Frog

Mary had a five-foot frog
That was very, very edgy
She took it to school one day
And her teacher got a wedgie.

All the boys started to laugh
And the girls began to giggle
They didn't notice the pet got out
Until the teacher's pants began to wiggle.

Richard Tolson (10)
Lytchett Matravers Primary School, Poole

Countries

In the USA I would love a 2ft hot dog, *yum!*
In France I would like to try snails, *yuck!*
In Australia I would adopt all the animals apart from
Snakes of course!
In the North Pole I will build an igloo, cold.
In Canada I would go sightseeing, *wow!*
You don't know how much I want to see the
                    World!

Hannah Maese (9)
Lytchett Matravers Primary School, Poole

The Environment

Grass so green with the sun shining on it.
Trees growing from magnificent, glorious rain.
Flowers poking their heads out of the ground.
No soil won't survive, flowers need soil to grow.
Flowers growing, flowers dying.
Dreadful bombs dropping and destroying the environment
But it all grows back again
To make a lovely view from up above.

Rebecca Tummon (8)
Lytchett Matravers Primary School, Poole

Lights, Camera, Action

Lights flash,
I watch the stars twirl around,
Glitter sparkles in the light,
Hilary starts to sing her song,
The boys and girls madly clap,
Some cameramen shout out, 'Bravo!'

Cameras click,
A shout demands, 'Cut,'
Movie is the thing they want,
'Ellie please don't leave,'
Rolly begins to bark,
A voice then says, 'Where is that Mart?'

Acting is such hard work,
'Come on Ellie, do your best,'
Time is passing very quickly,
It's almost time to go.
Onward we plod,
Now it's time to end the day, so, 'Bye!'

Charlotte Ettling (10)
Lytchett Matravers Primary School, Poole

Underwater

I fall off a boat into the sea,
Look behind me, what do I see?
A great white shark following me,
I swim, I swim, oh how I swim,
I look behind me, I can't see him.
I swim right up to the surface,
I still can't see him,
But I see a dolphin and jump up to greet him.
I shake his fin and say hello,
Then I swim away, after waving.

Mollie Heap (8)
Lytchett Matravers Primary School, Poole

Football!

Football is full of surprises,
And all sorts of curious laws
Like holding your bits
When taking free kicks
And kissing each player who scores.

Man U are the best, some will disagree
Arsenal are the worst, I bet some will agree.
Chelsea are alright
But when the ball comes, Lampard gets a fright!

I like to play football
I don't like red, yellow fouls
But I also like climbing a wall
But I like our football towels!

Louis Castle (10)
Lytchett Matravers Primary School, Poole

Six Rolling Waves

The first wave was called Rolling Wave,
He swallowed some seaweed and was never seen again.
The second wave was called Greedy Wave,
He ate too many fish and splash, he burst.
The third wave was just plain stupid and bumped into a rock, *bang.*
The fourth wave was *sooo* posh that she realised you could see
Straight through her and thought she was naked and sailed away.
The fifth wave was called Fast Fred and he went so fast he couldn't
See the fishing net and got sliced into pieces.
The sixth wave was so clever because it was a race,
He rolled all the way to shore,
And was carried out to the glittering sea,
Only to start the journey again.

Georgina Hart (9)
Lytchett Matravers Primary School, Poole

Mary Had A . . .

Mary had a warty frog,
She took it to the park,
It jumped into the pond one day,
And was eaten by a shark.

Mary shouted at the shark,
And screamed at it like Hell,
She jumped into the pond with it,
And was eaten up as well!

A fisherman came and set the hook,
Amongst some weeds like lace,
But when he caught a great fat shark,
You should have seen his face!

He cut the shark meat down to bone,
And there inside the ribs,
Was Mary and her little frog,
Sat reading Jamie Tibbs!

Sam Scriven (10)
Lytchett Matravers Primary School, Poole

Weather

The rain is so annoying
It pitter-patters all over the ground
Wherever I go it always rains
Oh no, oh no, it has started to rain again
I might as well go home.
The sun is so hot
It shines in your eyes all the time
The wind blows the trees and blows the bushes.
Storms are frightening at night
In the parks, on the ground
Always going *bang, bang!*
In the fog you cannot see.
Stamp, stamp! What is that?
There's something tickling my back.

Andrew Hillman (8)
Lytchett Matravers Primary School, Poole

Football Crazy

David Beckham places the ball
But after he needs to get it over the wall

His teammate Zidane plays in any role
No matter what, he scores a goal.

Goal buster Rooney never has a rest
He reminds me of that legend George Best.

Hard nut Roy Keane is pretty bright
But he always has to start a fight.

Ronaldinho is so brill
His goals are such a thrill.

Buffon is a star goalie
He saves them by doing a roly poly.

Roberto Carlos is really small
You got to admit his free kicks rule.

Taylor Broom   (9)
Lytchett Matravers Primary School, Poole

My Go-Kart

I have a go-kart,
I ride it around
It's not very fast
And it doesn't stay
On the ground.

It does big flips and
Knocks off bits
Such as wheels from prams
And bolts from trams.

Michael Prince   (10)
Lytchett Matravers Primary School, Poole

Fairy Tales

The dragon's flame
The scream of a dame
The flash of armour
The magic charmer,
The fairy's wings
The siren sings.

The witches' spell
The goblins smell
The unicorns fly
The leprechauns sigh,
The mermaids wish . . .

These are the magical creatures!

Ellen Taylor (10)
Lytchett Matravers Primary School, Poole

Scary Teachers

Scary teachers
They haunt the school
Anyone who enters
Becomes a ghoul.

Ghoulish gardeners
They haunt the park
Anyone who played football
Becomes a shark.

Shark-like shopkeepers
They haunt the shop
Anyone who buys something
Gets the chop.

Matt Burton (10)
Lytchett Matravers Primary School, Poole

Snails And Slugs

Slow, slimy, shiny snails,
All across the wet pavement,
Be careful where you step,
Or there will be a terrible mess!

Slow, slimy, shiny slugs,
All fat or skirpy on the wall,
They are slower than snails,
But they are fun to watch.

Slow, slimy, shiny snails and slugs
Slowly cross the path,
Leaving slimy trails,
When I put some lettuce out,
It's gone in just ten seconds!

Slow, slimy, shiny snails,
You see them everywhere you go,
On the coasts, in the wood,
Even in your backgarden.

Slow, slimy, shiny slugs
Live under stones,
And under the ground,
They don't live in water because they will drown!

Slow, slimy, snails and slugs,
Up rises the sun,
And soon they're all out of sight,
That's because they're nocturnal.

Slow, slimy snails and slugs
Come out tonight again,
To leave their slimy trails,
And to show their shells and bodies!

Hollymay Gladwin (10)
Lytchett Matravers Primary School, Poole

9.00

Ring, ring, ring, goes the bell,
All the shouting stops,
To give the teacher time to yell,
'Go and line up!'

Year 6 in the big playground,
Year 5 separated,
Year 4 by the mobiles,
Year 3 nearby,
Year 2 in the small playground,
Year 1 by the post,
Reception by their classrooms,
The nursery eating toast.

Ring, ring, ring, goes the bell,
Register time is here,
Acting as if they are in a spell,
Calls of *yes* from everywhere,
And cursing as well!

Early years working,
English, maths, science,
Older years listening,
Assembly time: awards.

Ring, ring, ring, next lesson,
Early years listening,
Assembly, fun, games,
Older years working,
Boring, asleep annoyed.

Ring, ring, ring, goes the bell,
All the shouting starts,
This is going to turn to Hell,
Headaches everywhere.

Abbey Butterworth (9)
Lytchett Matravers Primary School, Poole

Mary Had A . . .

Mary had a little tiger
She thought it was quite cute
But when she shouted at it one hundred times
It went into mute.

Mary did not know what to do
It would not growl at all
She took it to the vet one day
And it started chasing a ball.

Mary ran right after it
But she got tired on the way
She tripped over a stick again
And went into a bundle of hay.

The tiger stopped and sniffed around
To look at poor Mary on the ground
Then the tiger started running back
Then ate Mary, so she's not around.

Stefan Webster (10)
Lytchett Matravers Primary School, Poole

Animals That Keep The Farm Running

There's . . .
A cat to catch the vermin mouse
A chicken to lay the speckled eggs
A cow to give the creamy milk
A horse to plough the fields of course
A pig for the general jig
A sheep to keep in charge for Little Bo Peep
A dog to catch Doctor Frog
But isn't it amazing what animals do on farms these days.

Toby Wonnacott (10)
Lytchett Matravers Primary School, Poole

Summer

Summer is a time of joy,
When every little girl and boy,
Goes to the seaside for some fun,
And there their mothers rest in the sun.

Boys surf and girls bathe,
But their mothers say, 'Do behave.'
They then behave as good as gold,
Until the time comes when they are told.

To fold the chairs up from the beach,
After having a bite of peach,
They go home to have their tea,
And they will return to the sea.

Katie Dechow (10)
Lytchett Matravers Primary School, Poole

My Family

My family is great, I know it's true
My mum is so good, you could be too.
My dad is scary, my sister is too
They do big parties, a Hallowe'en one too.
My dad is so lonely, but in summertime we have fun.
Yes, yes, we did have to run.
In wintertime, Mum cooks great soup
Yum, yum, it's getting dark.
I jump into bed and say goodnight.

Lacy Dominey (8)
Lytchett Matravers Primary School, Poole

Tears

I have two eyes
I have a nose
I have brown hair
And wrinkly toes
I have a head
I have pink lips
I have two feet
I have two hips
I have two hands
And two ears
I have two arms
And I
 Cry tears!

Emily Atkinson (10)
Lytchett Matravers Primary School, Poole

Old Little Fish

Old Little Fish went to space in a rocket,
Flew through the asteroid belt,
Saw a monster then hid in his pocket!

Old Little Fish landed on Mars,
Saw a mean, mean alien,
Got scared, then he ate chocolate bars!

Old Little Fish got burnt on the sun,
'Ouch, ouch, ouchies,' he screamed,
So it was hot enough to cook a hot bun!

Andrew Sofianos (10)
Lytchett Matravers Primary School, Poole

Strawberries

Red, gleaming, yummy strawberries,
Always eaten by me,
Hundreds picked out of the ground,
Red, gleaming, yummy strawberries.

Red, gleaming, yummy strawberries,
Constantly always eaten by Mum,
Soon they'll be all gone,
Red, gleaming, yummy strawberries.

Red, gleaming, yummy strawberries,
Baby Izzy squashed them,
No wonder they were all gone,
Red, gleaming, yummy strawberries.

Red, gleaming, yummy strawberries,
Gone in ten seconds,
Yum, yum, yum,
Red, gleaming, yummy strawberries.

Gemma Hart (10)
Lytchett Matravers Primary School, Poole

Teachers

Mrs Cotterill is talkative
Mrs Sandel is laughable
Mr Dorrel's maths is just about manageable
Miss Bowditch is sensible
Mrs Lewis is very likeable.

Teachers, teachers, teachers, teachers,
Some are good, and some are bad,
Some are happy, some are sad.

Jodie Peters (10)
Lytchett Matravers Primary School, Poole

Pets

I have a floppy dog,
All he does all day is jog,
I know that he thinks he's cool,
But sometimes he can be a fool.
My cat loves to catch lots of rats,
But I would just use a baseball bat,
I think it's harder than he thinks,
I bet that's why he always sinks!
Bob my fish is sometimes quite scary,
He glows up at night and goes all hairy,
He swims all day,
With his friends he likes to play.
My python rat,
Likes to chew a rounders bat,
She chews and chews,
When she's finished, trust me, it doesn't look new!

Katie Gillion (10)
Lytchett Matravers Primary School, Poole

Cats And Kittens

Cats and kittens, similar things
They like to play with a lot of odd things.

Cats and kittens with long fluffy fur,
I like to hear a purr occur.

Cats and kittens cough up fur balls
As they paddle down the hall.

Cats and kittens chase each other,
While their mother lazily sleeps.

Louisa Styles (10)
Lytchett Matravers Primary School, Poole

The Dragon

D ragons are large with lots of scales
R otting teeth and long, dirty nails
A pair of wings that lifts it higher
G reat big jaws that breathe out fire
O ver go the gate and rail,
kN ocked by its great big tail
  S o don't go anywhere near a dragon,
    You don't want to get knocked over.

Megan Alexander (9)
Lytchett Matravers Primary School, Poole

Mum

Mum
Mums love their children
Loving, caring, bossy
Like a lion caring for its cubs
Like bodyguards looking after a VIP.

I feel loved
Mum
Makes me think how lucky I am.

Jack Hammond (10)
Meeching Valley Primary School, Newhaven

Poppy

What if I was in the war
Retreating from guns and death
An explosion in front of me
Blinding me to the ground
Not knowing which way to go
Wishing I was safe.

Liam Dolan (11)
Meeching Valley Primary School, Newhaven

The Bully

Steals, lies, injures, cowardly, horrible, immature
Like a bull going for its target.
I feel upset.

The bully.
Use its strength against someone
Who is weaker than them
They have a problem
He lies to people horrible, terrifying, scary, nasty, ugly
Scary as a bull
I feel terrified
The bully
My dad getting angry.

Alice Fuller (10)
Meeching Valley Primary School, Newhaven

Mother

Gave birth to me
Bossy, caring, loving
Like a rainbow shining over me
Like a nurse caring for her passion
I feel safe, safe as money in a box,
Lock up and throw away the key
Mother reminds me how loving mums can be.

Katrina Matthews (11)
Meeching Valley Primary School, Newhaven

Night

Night
Dark
Cold, scary, goosebumps
As dark as being in a gun
As black as shadows
I feel frightened.

Richard Taylor (11)
Meeching Valley Primary School, Newhaven

Tsunami

Tsunami,
Kills thousands of people,
Horrendous, destroying, terrifying,
Like a wave covering up the whole world,
As destructive as the plague,
I feel scared,
As scared as a person losing their home,
Tsunami,
Reminds us how short life can sometimes be.

Laura Coley (11)
Meeching Valley Primary School, Newhaven

Tsunami

Massive tidal wave
Horrendous atmosphere
Like a volcano erupting
As destructive as a fire
I feel scared
I feel as scared as a bird that has lost its egg.
Tsunami
Reminds us how lucky we are.

Natasha Parton (11)
Meeching Valley Primary School, Newhaven

Tsunami

Huge tidal wave.
Terrifying, horrendous, devastating.
Like a steamroller in a glass shop.
As destructive as the plague.
I feel petrified.
I feel as exposed as a worm on the ground.
Tsunami.
Reminds us how destructive nature can be.

Oliver Barron-Carter (11)
Meeching Valley Primary School, Newhaven

What If?

What if that was me
Lying in the trench
Blood dripping down my face
In agony and pain
What if that was me?
Marching down the road
Fighting for my country
Not knowing what was going to happen
So please remember them who fought for us that day.
11.11 the scariest day of all.

Emily Cornford (11)
Meeching Valley Primary School, Newhaven

The Bully

The bully
Hurts, fights, backchats, destroys
Cruel, horrible, disrespectful
Like a bulldog picking its next target
I feel terrified
The bully
Reminds us what people can be like.

Hannah Deakin (10)
Meeching Valley Primary School, Newhaven

Tsunami

A horrendous earthquake killed hundreds of people in Asia
People were terrified of the tidal wave, they also lost all of their food
Their homes have been destroyed,
The tidal wave was so powerful it even dragged little children
As well as their mums and dads to their death.

Josh Sarrou (11)
Meeching Valley Primary School, Newhaven

Tsunami

Enormous destructive wave
Dashing, terrifying, worrying,
Like a dog chasing a cat into the house
As scary as a ghost
I feel in danger
I feel terrified as a fish being chased by shark
Tsunami
Reminds us how destructive nature can be.

Rebecca Kite (11)
Meeching Valley Primary School, Newhaven

Tsunami

Massive destructive wave
Nerve-racking, life crushing, bones broken
Like Bruce Lee punching
As destructive as a nuclear bomb
I feel silenced
I feel as lost as a pebble on the shore
Tsunami
Reminds us how short life is.

Sebastian Saunders (11)
Meeching Valley Primary School, Newhaven

War

Soldiers are saving us
Old, upset, scared
They might not like it, they don't want to die
Like a knife going through your head
I feel scared
As scared as a person riding a skateboard for the first time
Soldiers
I wonder if my grandad died in the war?

Emma Rix (11)
Meeching Valley Primary School, Newhaven

Tsunami

Tsunami
Massive tidal wave

Destroying, heartbreaking, terrifying,
Like a humungous surfing wave
As destructive as a gunshot
I feel scared
I feel as exposed as a little fish in the sea
Tsunami
Reminds us how precious life is.

Kadie Wright (11)
Meeching Valley Primary School, Newhaven

My Magic Box

(Based on 'Magic Box' by Kit Wright)

In my magic box I will put . . .
A fire breathing dragon
With large red wings.

I will put in my box . . .
A sharp, pointed vampire's tooth
With venom at the tip.

I will put in my box . . .
An electric snake
With a lion's claw.

I will put in my box . . .
The flick of a dolphin's tail
And a cheetah's fast legs.

My box is made of glittering,
Sparkling shiny gold
With blue sea waves
And a sabre tooth
My sabre tooth's colour
Is going to be dark black.

Chevron Phillips-McLean (9)
Park Hill Junior School, Croydon

The Magic Box

(Based on 'Magic Box' by Kit Wright)

I will put in the box . . .
The dazzling spark of a hammer forming a sharp sword,
The nervous energy of a daring acrobat.

I will put in the box . . .
The roar of a waterfall racing down to its bottom,
A parrot mimicking me.

I will put in the box . . .
The last word spoken by an ancient pharaoh,
The first sound of a newly born baby.

I will put in the box . . .
The happiest memories of my mind,
And the fiery breath of a Chinese dragon.

My magic box is made of . . .
The best gold made for me,
And the finest silk ever woven.

Callum Mance (8)
Park Hill Junior School, Croydon

The Magic Box

(Based on 'Magic Box' by Kit Wright)

I will put in my magic box . . .
The dangerous smell of a volcano erupting,
The spark of an electric guitar,
The feeling of the wind pushing the sea to make waves,
The sound of the people's voices.

My magic box is made of . . .
Dry clay sprinkled with glitter,
It has a sign of a wand in the middle.

In my magic box I shall put . . .
Lots of new, dangerous things.

Matthias Comrie (8)
Park Hill Junior School, Croydon

In My Magic Box

(Based on 'Magic Box' by Kit Wright)

In my magic box . . .
I will put in my box an ancient staff of Greek gods,
A mysterious and foggy island
A pyramid that appears in the dark.

In my magic box . . .
I will put crystals that lead you to darkness
And never end
The last words spoken in Hell.

In my magic box . . .
I will put the final shot of a football match
The last cheer of the crowd
A killer ghost of football.

In my magic box . . .
I will put the first bite of a mouth
The last laugh of an old woman
The most evil beast from Hell.

I will put in my box . . .
The first vortex on Earth
The tombs of Egypt
The first knight to slay a dragon.

In my box . . .
I shall hear the hunting of a mummy
The screaming of a great pharaoh dying.

Shuoh-Fuu Tang (9)
Park Hill Junior School, Croydon

The Magic Box

(Based on 'Magic Box' by Kit Wright)

I will put in the box . . .
The golden glow of the setting sun,
The sweet songs of birds in the newborn day,
The rich taste of golden honey.

I will put in the box . . .
The clap of thunder in an electrical storm, up in the heavens,
The calming flow of a sapphire stream,
The cheerful chirp of an active chipmunk.

I will put in the box . . .
The first breath of a clean soul,
The oldest stories the elderly know,
The gentle smile of a caring mother.

I will put in the box . . .
A new colour only I have seen,
A shimmering pearl as black as death,
And the scalding fires of Vesuvius.

My magic box is made of . . .
All the flower petals in the world,
The sun and the moon make the lid,
And in the corners are fragments of a shattered rainbow.

In my magic box I shall . . .
Hold a cloud in my hands,
Freely gallop on an emerald horse,
Drift on a water lily in a crystal pond.

Aliya Ismailova (8)
Park Hill Junior School, Croydon

The Magic Box
(Based on 'Magic Box' by Kit Wright)

In my magic box I will put . . .
The energy of someone running the marathon,
The whisper of the wind in the summer sun.

In my magic box I will put . . .
The light of the golden sun at dawn,
The spray of the Angel Falls.

In my magic box I will put . . .
The last wish of Rameses III,
The funniest poem of a famous poet.

In my magic box I will put . . .
The twinkling light of a distant star,
The pull of the heaviest black hole.

My magic box is made of . . .
Carved moon rock,
It has ice hinges.

In my magic box I shall . . .
Go into the distant future,
Build the best car ever invented.

Aman Berry (9)
Park Hill Junior School, Croydon

The Magic Box
(Based on 'Magic Box' by Kit Wright)

I will put in my magic box . . .
The starry night sky with the moon shining and the midnight breeze.
The birds which sing and flutter.

I will put in my magic box . . .
The sound of a stream swirling around and the fish which jump and
swerve,
The taste of chocolate swirling and swishing in my mouth.

My box is made of . . .
Parrot's feathers and bones.

Declan Card (9)
Park Hill Junior School, Croydon

The Magic Box

(Based on 'Magic Box' by Kit Wright)

In my magic box I will put . . .
The sound of the waves at the beach,
The yellow sun in the sky.

In my magic box I will put . . .
The whales in the crystal sea,
The electric spark of a thunderbolt.

In my magic box I will put . . .
The taste of rich chocolate.

My magic box is made of . . .
The bark off of a tree,
Feathers off of a tropical bird.

In my magic box I shall put . . .
The sound of the sea swishing and splashing.

Elizabeth Hillier (9)
Park Hill Junior School, Croydon

The Magic Box

(Based on 'Magic Box' by Kit Wright)

In my magic box I will put . . .
The rich smell of a rose in summer,
The sound of birds singing in summertime.

In my magic box I will put . . .
A lion's roar,
A rainforest full of fresh fruit.

In my magic box I will put . . .
Happiness of people laughing
The sadness of people crying.

My magic box is made of . . .
Sapphire and rubies which sparkle in the cool moonlight.

In my magic box I shall . . .
Keep lots of secrets that no one will ever discover.

Luke Adams (9)
Park Hill Junior School, Croydon

The Magic Box

(Based on 'Magic Box' by Kit Wright)

In my magic box I will put . . .
The first ray of sunlight hitting the Arctic ice,
The singing of blue whales in the Pacific Ocean,
A hint of the sun's nuclear core,
The hitting of a blacksmith's hammer against a red hot sword.

I will put in the box . . .
The last breath of a dying man,
The energy of a sprinting Olympic racer,
The fast beating of the human heart.

My magic box is made of . . .
The finest wood ever carved,
Coated in fire and ice.

In my magic box I shall . . .
Leap on the Arctic ice,
Fight great battles and bring my army to victory,
Gaze at the magnificent blazing sun.

Gil Yehezkel (9)
Park Hill Junior School, Croydon

The Magic Box

(Based on 'Magic Box' by Kit Wright)

In my magic box I will put . . .
The smell and sight of a sulphur spring,
The sound of crashing waves in the crystal sea.

In my magic box I will put . . .
The voice of a singing dolphin,
The taste of lovely chocolate.

My magic box is made of . . .
Shells from the sea and feathers from wild exotic birds.

In my magic box I shall . . .
Surf and swim in the turquoise silky sea.

Stephanie Eid (9)
Park Hill Junior School, Croydon

The Magic Box
(Based on 'Magic Box' by Kit Wright)

In my magic box I will put . . .
The sight of a football team scoring,
The smell of a tasty dinner and
The sight of people playing happily.

In my magic box I will put . . .
The bluest blue whale spraying its water spout as high as it can.
A cheetah zooming, running super fast,
A lion chasing you!

My magic box is made of . . .
A tree's bark,
And decorated with parrots' feathers.
The inside is as blue as the sky, with rubies which gleam.

In my magic box I shall put . . .
Melodious sounds of a thousand robins,
And the happy sound of children playing in the snow.

Victor Mendon (9)
Park Hill Junior School, Croydon

The Magic Box
(Based on 'Magic Box' by Kit Wright)

In my magic box I will put the sound of the rolling waves,
Crashing onto the sandy, smooth shores.

In my magic box I will put the loud sound of the music
From the lit up pier.

In my magic box I will put the joyful sound of children laughing
On the pier.

My magic box is made of a rainbow, all twirled up,
So that everything stays in it.

In my magic box I shall put the dreams of everybody
In the entire world.

Amal Nadeem (8)
Park Hill Junior School, Croydon

My Magic Box

(Based on 'Magic Box' by Kit Wright)

I will put in my box . . .
A hot beach full of scorpions
The sloping path of a sloth deep in the rainforest
The first frosty snowflake from a cold winter's day.

I will put in the box . . .
A giant wolf that could eat the world
A key to another dimension
And the whole world.

I will put in the box . . .
A glittery pyramid from Egypt
A sparkling golden sword
And a king's head.

I will put in my box . . .
The smell of gladiator's blood
The biggest dragon ever made
A vampire's tooth.

My box shall be made of . . .
Crystals as big as a mountain
Gold which is as bright as the sun
Emeralds from the evergreen tree.

In my box I shall put . . .
A night made of flames
Van Gogh's ear
And a shiny coin.

Nikhil Patel (8)
Park Hill Junior School, Croydon

The Magic Box

(Based on 'Magic Box' by Kit Wright)

I will put in my box . . .
A universe of pretty planets,
The tropical birds with beautiful wings to fly,
The whole face of the Earth.

I will put in my box . . .
The past, present and future,
Scaly dragons from the past,
And the fantastic animals from the deep blue sea.

I will put in my magic box . . .
The prehistoric land from the past
The first tear to fall
All the beautiful suns and moons.

I will put in my magic box . . .
A broken racket hit by 2000 asteroids
A wizard's wand, three taps and magic is created
And the God of Atlantis.

My box will be made from . . .
The shiniest gold ever known
Hard hinges for the sides
And the tusks of an almighty elephant.

In my box I shall . . .
Swim in the deepest ocean
Walk with dinosaurs
And walk into the biggest war the world has ever known.

Ryan Doherty (9)
Park Hill Junior School, Croydon

My Magic Box

(Based on 'Magic Box' by Kit Wright)

I will put in my box . . .
A tropical island that only I can see,
And a glittering diamond that you can see a mile away,
And I could be in a land of my own that no one knows.

I will put in my box . . .
A land of chocolate that I could eat,
A land full of fairies which I could play with,
And the longest veil for a white wedding.

I will put in my box . . .
My secrets that no one will now,
A photo of me as a baby,
And first baby tear.

My box will be made of . . .
Crystals from a magic cave.

In my box I will . . .
Be a world famous surfer,
And surf the seven seas,
And be a gold medallist.

Abbey Mason (9)
Park Hill Junior School, Croydon

The Magic Box

(Based on 'Magic Box' by Kit Wright)

In my magic box I will put . . .
A magical feeling of the wind touching my skin,
The sound of birds singing in their straw nests,
The sparkling glint of my family's eyes.

In my magic box I will put . . .
The sound of fish splashing in the water,
A snowman melting in the sun,
The sea washing onto the seashore.

In my magic box I will put . . .
My first baby words and my first step,
The first Egyptian mummy in the world,
My first friend at nursery.

In my magic box I will put . . .
The flash of a sparkling green traffic light,
All the secrets I ever had,
My first great day of school.

My magic box is made of . . .
Pure gold with green emeralds decorating the sides,
It has a crystal lock with a key to match.

Joy Docherty (8)
Park Hill Junior School, Croydon

My Magic Box
(Based on 'Magic Box' by Kit Wright)

I will put in my box . . .
Five golden feathers from the fastest eagle in the world.
The calm and gentle sea.
Some ancient bandages from an Egyptian mummy.

I will put in my box . . .
1000 wishes
A warm sandy beach.
All the mountains in the universe,
Two gigantic whales.

I will put in my box . . .
Three sharp knives
Twenty sparkly suns,
A baby's chin,
The heavens up in space.

I will put in my box . . .
A magic forest,
I will put in my box a hairy princess laughing.

My box is made of ice
With gold stars on the lid
Fairy dust in the corners
And dragon's blood on the side.

In my box . . .
I will swim in the gentle sea
I will use a hundred wishes
I will climb the frosty mountains
I will sleep under the glowing moons.

Hannah Meah (9)
Park Hill Junior School, Croydon

My Magic Box

(Based on 'Magic Box' by Kit Wright)

I will put in my box . . .
The sharp tip of a tiger's claw and a monkey's tail, swinging,
Tops of pyramids,
A pharaoh's head.

I will put in my box . . .
Gold from the deep, deep mines,
The ear of Van Gogh,
The ink of a pen splattered on paper.

I will put in my box . . .
Dolphins splashing in the sea,
The sound of waves crashing on the beach,
The rustle of a tree's branches in a quiet forest.

I will put in my box . . .
The sound of chalk screeching on a white board
The sound of a hurricane smashing
Birds singing all day long.

My box will be made of . . .
Diamonds shimmering and glossy gold
Sparking silver
A tiger's tender skin.

In my box I shall . . .
Climb the tallest mountain
Ski the steepest slope
Run fastest across a long distance.

Robert Reid (9)
Park Hill Junior School, Croydon

My Magic Box

(Based on 'Magic Box' by Kit Wright)

I will put in my box . . .
The three sides of the old pyramids,
The body of an ancient pharaoh
The clothes of a blacksmith.

I will put in my box . . .
The head of a dragon
A sky of white doves
The deep blue sea.

I will put in my box . . .
A sword of an ancient samurai
The very first word of a baby when it's born
A book of joy from the library of Heaven.

I will put in my box . . .
An everlasting note of my dreams,
A big sandy beach,
A long surfing board.

My box shall be made from . . .
The softest, shiniest, shimmering gold
The best emerald in all of China,
The bluest sapphire from the sea.

In my box . . .
I shall surf on a dragon's head.

Zwelake Chibumba (8)
Park Hill Junior School, Croydon

The Magic Box

(Based on 'Magic Box' by Kit Wright)

I will put in the box . . .
The swish of a dolphin's tail,
The first bark of a newborn puppy,
And the sound of children playing in a playground.

I will put in the box . . .
A key to another world,
The first laughter of a newborn baby,
And the glittery wings of an unknown fairy.

I will put in the box . . .
The greenest leaf of a tall oak tree,
The fin of a baby fish swimming swiftly,
And the hot rays from the shining sun.

I will put in my box . . .
The loud sound of a noisy classroom,
The teardrop of a lonely girl,
And the shining silver sea moving swiftly side to side.

My box will be made from . . .
Silver and steel and the edges will be decorated
With shimmering silver and gold stars.

In my box I shall . . .
Surf the seas and get washed up on a magical island
And I will live there until I die.

Charlotte Fitzhugh (8)
Park Hill Junior School, Croydon

The Magic Box

(Based on 'Magic Box' by Kit Wright)

I will put in my box . . .
Gold coins from other countries
Van Gogh's beautiful paintings
Golden secrets that nobody will ever hear.

I will put in my box . . .
Beautiful coloured stones that are magical
A ladybird's delicate wing
Tutankhamen's best treasures.

I will put in my box . . .
Bookshelves brimming with Roald Dahl and Jacqueline Wilson
books.

The first snowflake of a crisp, cold winter's day
A baby's first words.

I will put in my box . . .
A playful golden labrador puppy,
The first promise ever made,
Tiny pieces of the beautiful shining sun.

My box will be made of . . .
Delicate pieces of Heaven
The prettiest, magical fairy wings,
The colours of the soothing sunset.

I shall surf in my box,
With the shimmering dolphins
Colourful fish swimming beneath me,
Friends and family behind on the beach.

Ria Ivens (8)
Park Hill Junior School, Croydon

My Magic Box

(Based on 'Magic Box' by Kit Wright)

I will put in my box . . .
The swish of the she dolphin in the shimmering sea
The raincoat of the rhino in a rainforest
The tooth of the first rabbit.

I will put in my box . . .
The shimmer of a sari
The silk of the sea
The fluff of a cloud.

I will put in my box . . .
The first fish in the sea
The scientist who invented tea
A spaceship purple and green

I will put in my box . . .
The scale of a multicoloured mermaid,
The fin of the first dolphin,
The crown of the first king.

My box will be made from . . .
Silky silver and gorgeous gold,
The crystals of a crown,
Sequence of the first sari.

In my box I shall . . .
Surf to see the first dolphin in the sea,
I will hunt in my box to find Henry VII's head,
I will find in my box the key to another world.

Maanasa Hari (9)
Park Hill Junior School, Croydon

The Magic Box
(Based on 'Magic Box' by Kit Wright)

In my magic box I will put . . .
The scrape of a monster's claw.

In my magic box I will put . . .
A castle made of brick.

In my magic box I will put . . .
The fire and flapping wing of a
Beautiful red dragon.

In my magic box I will put . . .
A hundred fish, swimming in the
Great sea with sharks.

The magic box is made of . . .
Gold and silver demands to guard the demons.

In my magic box I shall . . .
Surf on the biggest surfboard ever.

Shahrukh Kewal (9)
Park Hill Junior School, Croydon

My Magic Box

(Based on 'Magic Box' by Kit Wright)

In my magic box I will put . . .
The sharp pointy tip of a long red pencil lead.

In my magic box I will put . . .
The largest dot from a ladybird's wing.

In my magic box I will put . . .
A shiny starfish box full of shimmering seashells.

In my magic box I will put . . .
High and low musical notes from my favourite songs.

My magic box is made of . . .
A bed of hard, crusty leaves and with glittering snowballs
Falling to the ground.

In my magic box I shall . . .
Visit faraway France and eat pain aux chocolate for
Breakfast.

Ashley Moisan (9)
Park Hill Junior School, Croydon

The Magic Box

(Based on 'Magic Box' by Kit Wright)

I will put in my box . . .
A bite from the beak of the biggest bird on Earth,
A magical, mystical fire that heals any injury,
The great god Ra's heavily guarded brain.

I will put in my box . . .
A one of a kind picture of a gorgeous, giant griffin,
A rare black jewel from a dragon,
The first ancient arrow shot.

I will put in my box . . .
A complicated watch to travel through time,
The shiniest scale from a dinosaur,
The first chirrup from a yellow chick.

My box will be made of . . .
The biggest piece of silver in the universe,
An eye from George Washington,
The iceberg which sunk the Titanic.

In my box I will . . .
Travel to the boiling sun,
Quickly pick up a gigantic fireball and
Finally go back to Earth proud of myself.

Keisuke Kanda (9)
Park Hill Junior School, Croydon

My Magic Box

(Based on 'Magic Box' by Kit Wright)

I will put in the box . . .
A big cow flying over the moon
The first pyramid built by the Egyptians
The tallest tree in the world

I will put in the box . . .
A little fairy flying around
The biggest school in the universe
The biggest colourful ice cream scoop.

I will put in the box . . .
The most colourful bug in the world
The egg of a baby dinosaur
A huge rainforest with all its colourful creatures

My box is made of . . .
Warm, beautiful sand from a glorious beach
The edges are made of the claws from a bat
The box is covered in dried yellow leaves.

In my box I will . . .
Become a millionaire
Surf as fast as I can,
And take a trip around the world.

Jamie Campbell (9)
Park Hill Junior School, Croydon

A Special Box

(Based on 'Magic Box' by Kit Wright)

I will put in the box . . .
A winter's day with water as cold as ice,
A mountain as high as the sky,
A creature as small as a mouse.

I will put in the box . . .
A secret as big as a tree,
A rainbow as colourful as a ribbon,
A desert as hot as a sun.

I will put in the box . . .
A shimmering butterfly fluttering everywhere,
A teardrop from Heaven,
A sunflower painted by Van Gogh.

I will put in the box . . .
A shop flooded with teddies,
A heart full of love,
A Red Nose Day full of joy.

My box will be made of . . .
A blue sapphire which sparkling in the night sky,
A brooch that has a sign.

Aliya Christie (9)
Park Hill Junior School, Croydon

My Magic Box

(Based on 'Magic Box' by Kit Wright)

I will put in my box . . .
A book never written,
The first, frosty snowflake on the coldest winter's day,
The soft wave of a calm sea.

I will put in my box . . .
The first word that the wind blew,
The first country ever to be discovered,
The angry growl of a bear.

I will put in my box . . .
The warning of a lion,
The unusual petals of the first flower,
The first stitch on a wedding dress.

I will fashion my box from a . . .
Lion's tooth and a piece of silk,
Dust from a pixie and a spider's web,
The first drop of dew and a golden leaf.

I will act in my box . . .
And end up writing for a book
Never written.

Jessica Garner (8)
Park Hill Junior School, Croydon

The Magic Box

(Based on 'Magic Box' by Kit Wright)

I will put in the box . . .
The booming beat of a blissful heart,
The leap of a large lizard,
An unfound unicorn, its horn,
A shimmering wonder.

I will put in the box . . .
A tsunami that struck South Asia.
A part of the Amazon with the
Endangered red face monkey,
The last fisherman's hook with no blood.

I will put in the box . . .
A hot Pluto and cold Venus,
A rhino with a fin,
A dolphin with a horn.

I will put in the box . . .
The last laugh of an old woman,
A clump of cloud from the sky above,
A song from a bright bird.

My box is made of . . .
Clinging claws for the lock,
Leads of pencils for the base,
And green mint grass.

In my box I shall . . .
Surf the sky,
Get blown away to an unfound island,
And stay there until I die.

Preveena Kulaveerasingam (9)
Park Hill Junior School, Croydon

The Magic Box

(Based on 'Magic Box' by Kit Wright)

I will put in my box . . .
The blue ocean alive with splashing dolphins,
The slow pace of a sloth deep in the rainforest,
The first frosty snowflake on a winter's day.

I will put in my box . . .
The thunderous roar of a monster in a dark cave,
The laughter of a first born baby,
The glittery wings of a flower fairy.

I will put in my box . . .
The sharp tooth of a fierce tiger,
The first tear of a crying child,
A golden spaceship off to Mars.

I will put in my box . . .
A bird with sharp claws,
A tiger with wings,
A book with a fin,
A fish with a title.

My box is made out of . . .
Twinkling stars from the night sky,
Shiny gold as sparkly as a crystal,
Petals of sweet blooms.

In my box I shall . . .
Soar high in the sky,
Flown in gentle breeze,
To a land full of fairies,
And live happily ever after.

Keyura Raveendran (9)
Park Hill Junior School, Croydon

The Magic Box

(Based on 'Magic Box' by Kit Wright)

I will put in the box . . .
The lightest rain you ever have seen,
The most beautiful painting you have ever seen.

I will put in the box . . .
The light of the moon and stars,
A rainbow with all its colours.

I will put in the box . . .
A pharaoh's secret,
The sound of a beautiful song.

My magic box is made out of . . .
The scales of a Chinese dragon.

In my magic box I shall . . .
Fly to the distant past.

Taynila Gungaram (8)
Park Hill Junior School, Croydon

Solar System

S pace is as wide as an ocean
O rbit is as thin as a piece of string
L unar soil is as smooth as dust
A stronauts are as brave as knights
R ockets speeding like a cheetah.

S tars are as yellow as the sun
Y ellow stars twinkle like diamonds
S aturn is as orange as Tigger
T he aliens are as ugly as my brother
E arth is as round as a football
M ercury is as hot as a cooker.

Teiren Sugden (9)
Pickhurst Junior School, West Wickham

Treasure

I have something called treasure!
It is something you cannot measure,
It gleams with joy,
And it's as small as a toy!
Oh, it is something called treasure!

Oh treasure, oh treasure,
I have something called treasure!
It sparkles with glee,
It's as tall as a tree!
Oh, it is something called treasure!

I have something called treasure!
It is something like pleasure,
It's as fragile as glass,
And it's as big as Marble Arch!
Oh, it is something called treasure!

Pierce Grannell (8)
Pickhurst Junior School, West Wickham

The Death Of Che Guervara

Dear Mother,
I am awaiting execution for I was captured,
By US Operatives and Bolivians,
And about to be sent into oblivion,
The US were wearing green berets,
But luckily now they've caught me, I have no regrets.

I am scared that I'm about to die,
But I will be sent into the sky,
I hear them call my name,
I hope I have not brought you shame,
I hope my name will be said again.
Your loving son,
        Che Guervara.

Callum Carvell (11)
Pickhurst Junior School, West Wickham

The Time Capsule

(Based on 'Magic Box' by Kit Wright)

I will put in my time capsule . . .
The smell of sweet bubble bath,
The taste of melting, warm chocolate,
The sound of carol singing on Christmas Eve,
The feeling of a warm blanket on a cold night,
The vision of content children laughing as they play together.

I will put in my time capsule . . .
Bright, yellow daffodils sprouting in early spring,
The ice cream dripping down my chin in summer,
Crunching in freshly fallen snow in winter,
Falling leaves in late autumn.

I will put in my time capsule . . .
A cosy cuddle with my nana,
Before she tucks me up in bed.

I will put in my time capsule . . .
Televisions, computers and iPods
(Which we use for different things today).

My time capsule is full of wishes and dreams and secrets
In every corner.
My time capsule is filled with memories of all sorts,
Good and bad, happy and sad.
My time capsule is filled with fairy dust,
My time capsule is my own,
My time capsule is filled with magic to be revealed.

Hannah Badham (10)
Pickhurst Junior School, West Wickham

My Special Time Capsule

(Based on 'Magic Box' by Kit Wright)

In my time capsule I shall put . . .
The taste of fresh juicy strawberries,
The smell of beautiful roses
Also I shall put the sound of jolly laughing,
The sight of a newborn baby smiling,
And the touch of my cuddly teddy.

In my time capsule I shall put . . .
Autumn leaves floating down gently from trees.
Wonderful blossom off the trees in spring.
Soft crunchy white snow.
Summer sun which makes everything bright.

In my time capsule I shall put . . .
Mum and Dad's loving hugs which are like a giant shield around me.
Family dinners which bring us together.

In my time capsule I shall put . . .
A dream to have a long, nice, happy, long life,
An ambition to travel worldwide to funky jungles
And be a vet to loads of fantastic animals.

In my time capsule I shall put . . .
The mobile phone and the mind of a computer,
Which stores all the information in the world,
So in the far, far future, they know it all.

My time capsule is made from gold and painted with the elements
And lined with memories good and bad.

Josie Rendle (10)
Pickhurst Junior School, West Wickham

My Disco Dancing Rabbit

My pet rabbit likes to dance,
He likes to strut his stuff,
He dances all the way through the night,
Only stopping when I shout, 'That's enough!'

He moves along to the beat,
Bouncing, bopping and grooving,
He jigs and hops and makes strange noises,
Anything to keep him moving.

Whichever nightclub he goes to,
The female rabbits watch him from afar,
They think he is the grooviest rabbit,
They call him the 'Disco Star'.

At the end of the night when it is dark,
The rabbit knows he has danced too much,
He gets his coat and his scarf
And hops back home to his hutch.

Perry Noakes (10)
Pickhurst Junior School, West Wickham

A Day At The Beach

Ice cream, rock pools, sunshine and sand
Fairgrounds, amusements and big brass bands
A day at the beach what a great place to be
When I visit my nan who lives by the sea.

The water is freezing and salty and grey
With white horses crashing all round the bay
Boys on their surfboards with wet suits and flippers
Old men in deckchairs with sunhats and slippers!

The end of the day comes, the sun goes down
And bright lights appear all over the town
We walked along the front with our fish and chips
Tired and hungry licking our lips!

Rachel Penning (10)
Pickhurst Junior School, West Wickham

Why?

Why, oh why does my mum always moan?
I guess it's cos she knows best,
Whenever she enters my bedroom,
It's always in a terrible mess.

Why, oh why does my mum always moan?
I guess it's because she's in a mood,
I don't even have to ask her why?
It's because I haven't eaten my food.

Why, oh why does my mum always moan?
I guess it's cos she's trying to snooze,
And I've sneaked out to ride my bike,
And ruined my brand new shoes.

Why, oh why does my mum always moan?
I guess it's cos she knows best,
And when she shouts, *'Get to bed,'*
I know I've given her too much stress.

Why, oh why are mums so stressy.

Kristie Bird (10)
Pickhurst Junior School, West Wickham

My Dad

My dad is fat,
My dad is bald,
My dad never goes to the gym at all.

He's a bouncy castle,
He's a rocky mountain,
He's a mad alien,
He's a smiley face.

Sometimes he gets angry,
But I still love him, more than words can say,
He's the greatest dad that lives today.

Eve Meyerowitz (10)
Pickhurst Junior School, West Wickham

Yuri Gagarin

Dear Dad,
Right now I'm in space
327 km above the Earth,
Travelling at 27400kph
But I want to have my feet back on turf.

I'm a Russian colonel
And a cosmonaut
Cabin pressure rising
Airlock temperature at naught.

I'm as powerful as an iron bar
Brave, bold, noble and strong
I'm travelling really fast
But this journey's really long.

I'm in Vostok One now
Only 27 years old
With just me and the oxygen
I'm really cold.

I was born in Moscow
On a collective farm
My favourite place is Red Square
Oh how I miss its charm.

Love
    Yuri.

Alex Vale (10)
Pickhurst Junior School, West Wickham

Untitled

Dear Priscilla,
I've been away for about six months now
I've been making it big
Hitting the screens.

I have got the nickname king of rock and roll!
I've been rocking so hard at the concerts,
Especially for my song, Jailhouse Rock.
I am missing Graceland but will be back soon.

I'm as hot as fire
And ecstatic that I made it.
Everywhere I go I see my picture on covers of stuff,
Have you?

I wanna show the world, what I'm made of
And rock harder than anyone else!
The crowd just goes wild when I'm on stage
Tonight I will wear a white-studded costume
I hope to see you soon
Give my love to Lisa Marie
And of course to you from your hunk.

Thank you, thank you,
Very much
Love
Elvis.

Olivia Bennett (11)
Pickhurst Junior School, West Wickham

Untitled

Dear Mum,
I am missing you so,
The weather's been great though,
I've got a new hit, it's rock 'n' roll,
Priscilla's by my side, like my baby doll,
Lisa Marie is as pretty as ever,
I've brought a new suit it's made of leather.

The tension's rising,
The results may be surprising,
I hope you've heard my song Jailhouse Rock,
I brought you an expensive frock,
The money's coming in,
I'm on a roll,
My picture's on the front of every cover,
My songs are on every radio station,
My head is spinning like a rollercoaster,
In Graceland the lights shine
I have so much fan mail, pile after pile,
I've got round to reading one pile out of one hundred!
It's crazy! So much to read, so little time.

Hope you're well, give my love to everyone,
From your dearest son,
Elvis.

Nikita Ogston (11)
Pickhurst Junior School, West Wickham

The Man Whose Life Was His Treasure

A man sitting on a railway picking up stones,
Down came an engine who broke his bones.
A man took him to the hospital,
The man whose bones were broken
He never ever sat on a train
Because he got scared of them.
And so he never ever travelled again in his life.

Aman Ahmed (8)
Pickhurst Junior School, West Wickham

A Poem From Space

Dear Mother
At the moment I am in space,
I'm in my rocket and it isn't a race,
I'm the first man to do this and I'm very excited
It's been very tough but I've *fighted and fighted*,
I took off in April 1961
It's great and I'm having fun.

I'm writing to tell you that I love you so,
I had to go as you know
I'm missing you rather a lot,
It's your birthday soon and I haven't forgot,
Flying in space has been my ambition,
I'm writing this letter without repetition.

It's a dangerous job,
As I sit here and sob,
You're the best mother ever,
This is a record endeavour
I sit here in my seat,
Soon we will meet.

From
    Yuri Gagarin.

Daniel Sayer (11)
Pickhurst Junior School, West Wickham

Treasure

My family is my friend
They never drive me round the bend
They are very funny
And I love my mummy.

I love my family and they love me
We are all a happy family.

    Family is my treasure forever!

Lucy Nord (8)
Pickhurst Junior School, West Wickham

E=MC²

Dear Colleagues,
I have moved to America due to
The catastrophic death toll of Jews in Germany,
For I am a Jew,
And all the Jewish people I know,
Are being brutally murdered.
While in America
I have won a Noble prize,
Along with one million dollars,
For proving my,
Theory of relativity $E=mc^2$

I have also proved
That time travel is theoretically impossible,
For you can't take apart atoms and molecules
And put them back together again.

I am getting old though,
And my brain isn't what it used to be,
My hair is grey but soon,
I will try to achieve something harder.
People keep asking me questions,
It's difficult to take it all in.

I hope to go back to Germany after the war,
But nothing is for certain.
I hope I have inspired
Some people in my time,
To actually do something with their lives,
Because the higher you aim,
The greater you can be.

James Burgess (11)
Pickhurst Junior School, West Wickham

Emmeline Pankhurst

Dear Mama
I have recently found the WSPU,
We are called the Suffragettes,
The Government has jailed most of my members,
But to us they are no fret!

I am as brave and noble as a knight,
And we will keep fighting to the end,
We will win this Mama,
Our confidence will not descend!

Christabel is doing fine,
She's fighting here, right at my side,
I am oh so proud of her,
But I feel she's still sad her father died!

I miss you Mama, oh so much,
As we are so far apart,
At times it is so lonely,
And I miss your home-made jam tarts!

I, myself have become popular in prison,
But I don't care,
Even though it is not ladylike,
I was actually there!

Oh Mama don't you worry,
Christabel, Sylvia and me will be fine,
Just relax, I will survive,
When we win, it will be divine!

Remember Votes for Women!
Love
    Emmeline.

Nicola McEntee (11)
Pickhurst Junior School, West Wickham

The Sea

The glistening, shimmering sea
What a wonderful place to be
The waves slip and slide to and fro
To the wonderful place to be.

Most people say what a place,
When they go for a boat ride
They say hooray to the wonderful time
Of the sea.

The tropical fish swish through soggy seaweed
They watch out for sharks
And hide behind rocks
To the wonderful tune of the sea.

The most precious sea with pearls
In clams and the clams' shells go up and down
Their shells clatter
To the wonderful tune of the sea.

Jade Donaldson (8)
Pickhurst Junior School, West Wickham

Newton Genius

Dear my beloved brother,
An apple that was falling from a tree,
Made the spark that enlightened me.
I knew there was an invisible force,
How could I be so dumb it was gravity of course.
My brilliant brain the size of a cricket pitch,
Now it has made me extremely rich.
That one apple the starting point,
I have now filled that history joint.
Next of all a Newton meter,
Now I'm famous, see you later.
        Isaac Newton.

Samuel Lanckmans (11)
Pickhurst Junior School, West Wickham

Treasure

(Based on 'Magic Box' by Kit Wright)

I pull out of my box . . .
A sparkling red jewel
Glistening in the bright sunlight
With many colours reflecting
Off the walls onto its triangular faces.

I pull out of my box . . .
A pocket watch
Which my great grandad had
When he was twenty-five.
It is solid gold
With a compass built inside.

I pull out of my box . . .
A picture of all my friends
Playing football in the park,
For me to treasure in the future
As my memories of the past.

Conor Parry (8)
Pickhurst Junior School, West Wickham

Ewan McGregor

Dear Family,
George Lucus the director showed a Star Wars collector
Around the set.
We approved so George did not get upset.
Me and Hayden had a lightsaber duel,
I beat him, I rule!
In the script I kick Hayden into a pit of lava.
Now he's become the evil sith lord Darth Vader.
The last few days have been a dream
And Hayden Christensen treated me to ice cream.

Ewan . . .

Paul Graham (11)
Pickhurst Junior School, West Wickham

I Will Put In My Box

(Based on 'Magic Box' by Kit Wright)

I will put in my box . . .
A photo of me when I was a baby
When my parents were holding me
It will be a treasure for all to see.

I will put in my box . . .
A couple of China bears to comfort me.
A charm bracelet from when I was a baby
That I will keep forever.

I will put in my box . . .
A little crystal that is quite tiny
It is very shiny and sparkly
It has tinges of red, blue and green,
The best sparkle that you have ever seen.

I will put in my box . . .
A doll from the 1960s
It's been in our family for 16 years.
It's truly something special to me.
As a memory just for me to see.

Eleanor Sutherland (8)
Pickhurst Junior School, West Wickham

The Sea

The sea is a launching, lurching lion
Brown and brave
With his magnificent mane
Minute upon minute
Second upon second
The roaring racing rocks hit the shore.

But on quiet days in the sun
When the waves do not run
The sea is at rest and relaxing
All is calm and still
The sea sleeps silently.

Joe Morilla (9)
Pickhurst Junior School, West Wickham

Space

Astronauts looking for new places in space,
Waiting to put the planets back in place,
Shooting stars bright and beaming with light,
Soaring through the sky with all their might.

Pluto is just small,
Jupiter is not at all,
The sun is burning hot,
But Mars is definitely not.

Things floating all the time,
Out of the spaceship I climb,
Aliens coming out to chat,
Greeting me by taking off their hat.

Pluto is just small,
Jupiter is not at all,
The sun is burning hot,
But Mars is definitely not.

Victoria Munt (10)
Pickhurst Junior School, West Wickham

The Sea

The sea is a beastly, black bull
Black and ballistic is the bull
With his touchiest teeth
Day upon day
Week upon week
Go the whistling, wailing waves.

But on quiet days when it's warm
When waves are no fun
The sea is sweet and swift
All is soft and dreamy
And the sea slumbers in peace.

Siân Semerey (9)
Pickhurst Junior School, West Wickham

My Planets

Through my telescope I saw all
The planets in the sky.
The sky was black and way up high.
Mercury was the colour red,
And made me want to go to bed.
Venus was second in line,
And made me think of a grapevine.
Earth was number three,
Then I saw a bumblebee.
Next was Mars,
Which was surrounded by stars.
Jupiter was very big,
Then a bright blue alien started to dig.
Saturn had a ring,
Then the golden bells started to ding.
Uranus spinned on its side,
Which means my dad had lied.
The next one was Neptune
Which made me think of a baboon.
Pluto was very small,
And shaped like a ball.

Jazmine Wilkinson (10)
Pickhurst Junior School, West Wickham

Dinosaurs

Dinosaurs small, dinosaurs big,
We try to find their fossils so we dig and dig.

Dinosaurs thin, dinosaurs fat,
You might find their bones under a basement flat!

Dinosaurs in books, some on the telly,
Some are like my uncle,
Big, fat and smelly.

Some with big legs like tyrannosaurus,
Others with big eyes, do-you-think-he-saurus!

Oliver Saunders (10)
Pickhurst Junior School, West Wickham

Solar System

S hooting stars are like twinkling water
O n a rocket as fat as a cheetah
L una rocks glowing like the sun
A stronauts as brave as Superman
R acing comets as fast as running horses

S pace is as scary as a terrifying monster
Y ou see the Earth from space
  It's like a green and blue football
S olar sytem is like lots and lots of roads
T winkling stars are like millions of ants
E arth spinning like a hurricane
M illions of people watching rockets go into space
  Like shining eagles.

Alexzandra Vlahovic (10)
Pickhurst Junior School, West Wickham

Bobby Moore

Dear Bobby Charlton,
We won the World Cup,
I was captain of the team,
I worked them very hard, they thought I was very mean.
When we won the World Cup the feeling was great,
As our goals were really late.
The players were amazing, so were the fans,
The noises were like a million pots and pans.
People now admire me
Plus I got an OBE.
From your dear friend,
Round the bend,
    Bobby Moore.

Joe Darbourne (11)
Pickhurst Junior School, West Wickham

Anne Boleyn

Dearest Elizabeth,
The day I married King Henry,
I didn't stop to think for a titch,
That in a few years I'd be executed,
Because he thought I was a witch.

The public had rumours of a sixth finger,
Growing out of my right hand thumb,
Some even thought I had three breasts,
How stupid! How dumb!

I suppose though,
I should be blamed,
For my five affairs,
I'm truly shamed.

Oh dear Elizabeth,
Why did I act so foolishly,
To be accused of treason,
By his Majesty?

But I guess,
Like all sinners today,
The price of death,
I shall have to pay.

Cope with this bravely
Like I know you can,
Your scared, worried mother,
Anne.

Geneviève Zane (11)
Pickhurst Junior School, West Wickham

Polar Bear

The polar bear is like snow
He camouflages with his fur
He roars like the wind
As you've never heard before.
He is as hard as ice
The polar bear will charge at you
Like the coldness reaching your fingers
You will never spot him
His nice fluffy coat is like the softness
Of the snow melting as the sun goes down.

Emily Briant (9)
Pickhurst Junior School, West Wickham

Skeletons

One skeleton falling down,
Screeching down the wall like a howling wolf.
Two skeletons falling down,
Thudding like a shipwreck, falling on the seabed.
Three skeletons falling down,
Shattering like pieces of broken china.
Four skeletons falling down,
And I was screaming like an opera singer.
Then an avalanche of skeletons falling down,
Bumping and banging, like the beating of a drum.

Ben Card (8)
Pickhurst Junior School, West Wickham

Treasure Box

(Based on 'Magic Box' by Kit Wright)

I will find in the box . . .
A crystal painted with the colours of the wind.
A dancing fire jiving to jazz music,
The silky wings of a butterfly's flight.

I will find in the box . . .
A diamond found in the crevice of a rock
The heavenly breath of wind passing over a hill
A piece of script written in italic handwriting.

I will find in the box . . .
A clock whose numbers are Roman numerals
An oyster scented with the smell of the sea.

I will find in the box . . .
A piece of beautiful Roman pottery
A coin that was used in Victorian times
The cloth bandages of an Egyptian queen called Nefertiti.

I will find in the box . . .
A locket full of fairy dust
The music from a symphony orchestra
The sound of pianos ringing in my ears.

Faith Hawthorn (8)
Pickhurst Junior School, West Wickham

My Sister

My sister is a groovy girl
Who's everybody's mate.
She's brilliant and fantastic
She's really, really great.
She's there when you're lonely,
It's true she really is.
Her name is Rachel
She is the best sister ever.

Hannah Penning (7)
Pickhurst Junior School, West Wickham

Treasure Box

(Based on 'Magic Box' by Kit Wright)

In my box . . .
I have a clock
As delicate as a sparkling jewel
In the sunlight.

In my box . . .
I have a doll
As special as the stars
In the pitch-black sky.

In my box . . .
I have a smelling bear
Which is as white as a fluffy cloud
In the bright summery sky.

Eden Ansell (8)
Pickhurst Junior School, West Wickham

My Treasure

My treasure is
As sparkling as twinkling stars.
As long as an acorn tree
As big as a giant's house,
As round as a bouncy ball,
As colourful as a beautiful parrot,
As lovely as fairies' wings,
As glittering as golden diamonds,
As glistening as silver ice
What is my treasure?

Maria Martin (7)
Pickhurst Junior School, West Wickham

The Universe

T he universe is as big as an elephant
H oles, black holes as deep as a well
E veryone glimmers on the moon like a star.

U ranus is as blue as the sea,
N eptune is a wonderful planet,
I cy shadows we see on the moon as icy fingers on a window.
V enus is as round as a ball
E arth is as blue as a marble
R ockets fly like birds in the sky
S tars shimmer like diamonds
E nergetic astronauts soaring through space like a cheetah.

Lottie Ballard (10)
Pickhurst Junior School, West Wickham

Treasure

In my treasure chest there are . . .
Dazzling diamonds that sparkle all over
Smooth pearls, that twinkle in the wavy sea,
Rusty knives, that mean men use to rip open animals.
Beautiful shells, that were washed out to sea.
Shiny coins, that fell from a pirate's ship.
Crystal earrings that were treated very badly!
A pair of smelly socks, that have holes in the soles.
Golden lockets that have shared many memories.
There are lots of other things, but they are very secret.

Sarah Baldon (8)
Pickhurst Junior School, West Wickham

A Tragic Event

Through my telescope, I saw a massive meteorite heading to Earth,
But I was more worried about it hitting my mum's new turf.
A bright green alien was going to Mars,
While trying to avoid the shooting stars.
Then I suddenly remembered the meteorite all big and bold,
And wondered how it got into its gigantic mould.
How will it hit Earth is all I know?
Or maybe it will shrink and not grow.
But I will take a look once more at the deep blue sky
And wishing that I won't die!
So goodbye is all I can say,
And I can bet you £20 that I won't be here the next day.

James Lanckmans (10)
Pickhurst Junior School, West Wickham

The Angry Sea

The sea is growling, the sea is mad,
The sea is crashing, the sea is sad.
Why is the sea angry and why is the sea sad?
The sea is like an angry giant,
The sea is furious with anger,
The sea is crashing against rocks with temper,
The sea ships are slapping against the edges,
The sea is getting calmer, the sea is getting gentle,
The sea is howling at the wind because the sea
Wants to be peaceful and calm.

Lily Outram (8)
Pickhurst Junior School, West Wickham

The Universe

T he universe is as big as the world x by two million
H undreds of black holes as deep as a well
E agles as fast as the rockets going into space

U ranus is as round as a football
N eptune is as blue as the sky
I n a crater as big as a house
V enus is as orange as the sun
E arth is as blue as the sea
R ockets are as fast as a flash of lightning
S pace is as black as the bottom of a well
E veryone floats like a bird in the sky when they're in space.

Daniel Carpenter (10)
Pickhurst Junior School, West Wickham

Treasure

Treasure is silver,
Treasure is gold,
Treasure can be friends
Treasure can be family
Treasure can be pets
Treasure is dug up valuables
Treasure is China
Treasure is as shiny as the stars at night
Treasure makes you laugh
Friends make you laugh.

Emma Sullivan (8)
Pickhurst Junior School, West Wickham

My Time Capsule

(Based on 'Magic Box' by Kit Wright)

I will put in my time capsule . . .
The taste of sweet strawberries, swimming in smooth cream,
The smell of sweet, blooming flowers in the local park,
The purring of my friend's striped cat settling on my lap,
Seeing my family enjoying themselves at a party,
The cosy warm fur on my two favourite toys, I take to bed each night.

I will put in my time capsule . . .
My mum's sweet, soft smell,
My grandma's big, warm hugs,
My dad's loud cheer when there is a goal in a football match,
My brother's adventurous games that we play in the garden together.

I will put in my time capsule . . .
My dream to cuddle a polar bear,
An adventure to travel the world,
A memory never to forget,
The sight of my family after a day at school.

I will put in my time capsule . . .
Computers and mobiles and other modern things
That help us with our work today.

My time capsule will be old and rusty and made of tin,
But special and different to others,
As it would have been passed down the family for generations,
It will have a tiger's head engraved on the top,
My time capsule is magic, with history and secrets hidden away
                                                in the corners.

Ellen Simmons (10)
Pickhurst Junior School, West Wickham

Through My Telescope

Through my telescope I saw glittering stars
That were surrounding Mars.

A man was walking on the moon
As light as a fairy he was delicate and airy.

The stars were bright and filled the
Pitch-black night.

Through my telescope I saw a UFO, it flew past,
Really blurred, super fast.

A blazing sun where an alien was
Having lots of fun.

I saw a star on the run
Where an alien was eating a hot cross bun.

Victoria Smith (10)
Pickhurst Junior School, West Wickham

Through My Telescope

Through my telescope I saw,
Not just a few planets but lots more!

It looked like lots of different stars were having a race,
The most shiny star came in 1st place!

Jupiter, Saturn, Pluto and Earth,
Looked like they were playing football on turf!

When I went home it all stopped
All that time I realised it just popped!

Phoebe Blunt (10)
Pickhurst Junior School, West Wickham

In Space

In space, spaceships spin and fly,
Like jelly aliens which are spies.
In space there's a blazing hot sun,
And a bright sparkling moon,
And they both shine for you.
In space there are glittery stars,
And I saw a star zooming like a racing car.
In space there's tiny Pluto
But Jupiter is big though.

Amy Jardine (10)
Pickhurst Junior School, West Wickham

A Trip To The Jungle

All smells, good or bad
Birds singing all around
Leaves brushing on your face
Stomping on the grass
Plants all around.

Squirrel scurrying up a tree
Fox rushing all around.
Ponds all nice and clean.
Bark on all the trees
Branches flicking on your face.

Birds darting through the trees
Nettles pricking and annoying,
Stones hard at your feet.
Insects all around you
Litter spoiling nature.

Birds flying all around
Stumps just blend in,
Benches join the picture
Gates! Disgrace locking in nature.
This is the jungle.

Sean Sussex (9)
St Michael's Junior School, Aldershot

A Trip To The Jungle

It's quiet
It's lovely,
It's beautiful,
It's flowery.

There are wavy leaves,
There are spiky leaves,
There are smooth leaves,
There are rough leaves.

It's quiet,
It's lovely,
It's beautiful,
It's flowery.

There's white flowers,
Blue flowers,
Droopy flowers,
And baby flowers.

It's quiet,
It's lovely,
It's beautiful,
It's flowery.

There are stony paths,
Singing birds,
Trickling rain,
Surrounded by nature.

It's quiet,
It's lovely,
It's beautiful,
It's flowery.

It's the jungle!

Leah Paget (9)
St Michael's Junior School, Aldershot

Hunted

What can you see?
Alone in the darkness,
Calling out but knowing there'll be no answer,
Trapped and broken hearted.

Love has no meaning,
Scared in your own home,
Terrified to set foot outside,
Destroyed and unwanted.

Prowling eyes watching your every move,
Hands reaching into your life, tearing it apart,
Taking over your soul.

What can you feel?
Being turned against day and night,
Pain, torturing hope, beating love and kindness,
Blackness sucking you into a life of misery and unhappiness.

Tears burn at your eyes,
Fear lies in wait, waiting to pounce,
Waiting, to destroy your life!

Anger, bubbling up inside you, like a volcano ready to erupt,
Feelings, chained up inside, trying to escape.

What do you dream of?
A place to be safe, away from the dangers of outside,
The love of a *real* family.

The caring voice of a loving mother,
The laughter of a brother and sister,
No doors to trap me from thoughts,
The generosity of a kind father.

A life without terror.

Daisy West (9)
St Michael's Junior School, Aldershot

The Unwanted Boy

What can you see?
A boy sitting there unwanted,
Bullied and destroyed, threatened,
Nobody to care for him,
Terrified and frightened to walk through alleys,
Waiting for someone to come.

What can you feel?
I feel like turning back, fighting for myself,
Looking at every corner I look at and it's grey,
As darkness covers the sky,
Nobody to feel for you, instead they turn against you.

What can you hear?
Careful words spoken by his mother,
Gently cuddling him and a kiss on the head,
Saying, 'I will not leave you.'

Micheal Hayes (10)
St Michael's Junior School, Aldershot

A Fox In The Woods

The wood has a fox
And the ground crunches as he walks
Through the magical amazing place.
In the den the raindrops swirling,
Down in the tunnels where the fox sleeps.

Where he hunts is the woods,
Where the rabbit scuttles across the ground,
Where the badger strides in the dark.
And where the wind whistles.

The leaves get their colour
The pond gets its life.
The bee with its nectar humming
Goes where you feel free and happy.

Daniel Sullivan (9)
St Michael's Junior School, Aldershot

All Alone

What can you see?
A boy beaten and alone,
Unwanted and heartbroken,
People turning against me,
Threatened everywhere I go,
Sadness in my red blood streaked eyes,
A tear-stained face that will never leave me,
Wondering what happens next.

What can you hear?
Hear the banging of lockers,
Hear the footsteps chiming,
Thinking the bullies are coming towards me,
You can hear the screeches of children
Running away from their parents
And locking the doors behind them,
I can hear the moaning of the spirits searching for a victim.

Paige Powell (10)
St Michael's Junior School, Aldershot

A Jungle Safari

I'm going on a jungle safari
I wonder what I'll see?
Shall I tell you? OK
I saw some lovely darting birds all around me,
I saw a river that looked like the sea.

I'm going on a jungle safari
I wonder what I'll see?
Shall I tell you? OK
I saw some trees swaying and some bumblebees playing.

I'm going on a jungle safari
I wonder what I'll see?
Shall I tell you? OK
I saw some ladybirds flying out for their lunch,
When the leaves pop out they give me a punch.

Hannah Cole (9)
St Michael's Junior School, Aldershot

The Mystery Of Nature

Crispy, crunchy twigs,
The water glitters in the sun.
The mystery of nature, what wonderful things.
Feathers, nettles, all things of nature.
Foxes, badgers, darting birds, slimy slugs
All things of nature.
Smell that, what's that?
Look it's a flower.
Who created nature?
I wonder if God created all these things?

When it snows, everything grows.
The squirrel runs, making footprints.
The sly fox runs after it,
But the squirrel hides amongst the tiny flowers.
The fox goes home without any dinner.

The glittering water shines in the sun,
The newts swim peacefully,
The tadpoles sleep, while their mother keeps guard.
Soft, warm, cuddly feathers,
Sweet smelling, beautiful flowers,
Spiky, green stinging nettles.

God created all these things.

Layla Swindell (9)
St Michael's Junior School, Aldershot

The Torture Of Reality

What can you see?
Alone, travelling through darkness,
Unwanted, keeping tears for yourself,
Suffering in your own home,
Living a life of gloom,
Depressed in your petrified body.

Happiness turns to tears,
Beaten by gods of love,
Tortured by pain and defeat,
Destroyed by your own nightmare,
Evil steals your soul,
It wrecks your life.

What can you feel?
Fear gripping my lungs,
Like the prey of a lion,
Emotions flowing in my bloodstream,
The love is unwanted.

Footsteps come closer,
The bleak walls,
Trap me from reality,
Devils hunt my soul with anger,
Like a scream of a young girl.

Angels being bullied by grief,
Misery is in charge of love
Prowling eyes that watch me forever!

Rebecca Neve (10)
St Michael's Junior School, Aldershot

Sadness In The Deep

What can you see?
A boy beaten and alone,
Unwanted and broken-hearted,
Fear is in his eyes,
Tears upon his face,
Misery.

What can you feel?
A thousand knives inside, piercing my stomach,
Feeling unwanted everywhere I go,
Terrified to move, a thick grey mist around me.

What can I hear?
The sound of lockers banging noisily,
Shouting in the playground,
Kind words spoken from mother to son,
Footsteps coming towards me,
Heartbeats pounding faster and faster,
A place of safety in my heart.

Connor A Tomlinson (9)
St Michael's Junior School, Aldershot

The Wild Woodland

The quiet, peaceful place,
Trickling water in the pond,
Look up in the sky, blue and white meets your eye.
Brown, white, blue, yellow and red colours.
The sweet bird singing in the rustling trees.
The quiet bee buzzing in the air
The thin nylon carrying a spider
Water snail by a pond
The crunchy stick under your foot
Insects searching alone.

Tristan Tatarek (9)
St Michael's Junior School, Aldershot

Fear!

What can you see?
Unwanted and beaten to death,
Petrified of the world outside,
Fear gleaming in his eyes,
Lonely with no friends,
Mistreated.

What can you feel?
My heart has been ripped in two,
Grey clouds rain on me day and night.
A need to jump off a building,
Running millions of miles away, and forgetting everything.

What do you dream of?
The sound of a caring mum,
A gentle and loving family,
The laughter of a brother or sister,
The monsters to go away.

Kimberley Homer (10)
St Michael's Junior School, Aldershot

What Am I?

Oh you can't resist me,
I'm tasty and delicious,
I'll make your mouth water,
I'm brown and golden.
I'm creamy and tempting,
I'll dissolve in your mouth,
I'm smooth and I'm square,
I'm persuading you,
I'm fantastic and crunchy,
Crunch! Crunch!
(etalocohC)

Bryony Reed (9)
St Michael's Junior School, Aldershot

Bullied And Lonely

What can you see?
A boy sitting alone next to some lockers,
Mistreated and unwanted,
Left out and alone,
Destroyed and heartbroken.

What can you feel?
A need to run away,
My eyes are a tap I can't stop,
My lungs feel like they are being
Gripped by a lion attacking its prey,
Everywhere I turn there is darkness.

What can you hear?
Echoing voices whirling down the corridor,
The gentle voice of a mother as she speaks to her bullied son,
People smashing lockers,
Voices in my head saying, 'Help!'

Josh Ward (9)
St Michael's Junior School, Aldershot

Friends

Friends look after you
Friends tell you who's who
They play with you all day and everyday.

Friends make you happy
Friends make you laugh
They are kind at all times.

Friends look after you
Friends tell you who's who
They tell you lots more.

Kiran Anees (10)
St Michael's Junior School, Aldershot

Broken Hearted

What can you see?
Alone, in the darkness,
Threatened everywhere you go,
Calling out but knowing there will be no answer.

Beaten and depressed, too scared to step foot out of your own door,
Waiting for someone to come, wondering what will happen next?

What can you feel?
A need to run away, angry, a want for revenge,
Greyness everywhere I turn
I feel fear crawling up my spine like a spider.

What do you dream of?
People to stop beating me, to be able to walk out of my door,
Saying goodbye to people threatening me.

Happiness around me, no fear, no bullying,
For someone to love me, for the tears to go away.

Well that's only dreams!

Megan Paynton (10)
St Michael's Junior School, Aldershot

Dragons Aren't That Fierce

Everyone thinks that they should run
And put the bullets in their gun
Because people think that dragons are beasts
They think that dragons eat us for feasts
They say that dragons are nasty, you see
But they are legends and always will be
And nobody has ever before seen one
So how do they know that they should run?
And most of the people live in fear
Because all of the dragons that are near
But they are just as scared as you
And hide away, all but a few.

Camilla Haywood (11)
St Peter's Catholic Primary School, Shoreham-by-Sea

Why? Why? Why?

Birds fly . . . why?
Because they do . . . why?
So they can travel . . . why?
To find food . . . why?
So that they can eat . . . why?
So that they can survive . . . why?
Because they have chicks . . . why?
To continue the life cycle . . . why?
To that birds don't get extinct . . . why?
Because it would stop many other lifecycles,
As well as itself . . . why?
Because all the plants would die,
Because the birds carry the seed in their droppings,
So there wouldn't be any oxygen ah . . . why?
Oh I give up . . . why?
The end . . . why? Why? Why? Why? Why?

Joseph Sivver (11)
St Peter's Catholic Primary School, Shoreham-by-Sea

The Wrong Day

I woke up could it be,
The day that I had longed to see?
It was our residential trip today
I had to get ready straight away!
There wasn't any time to waste,
I had to hurry and make haste.
It was already half past eight
Oh no . . . I knew it, I was going to be late!
I quickly scurried out of the door
I couldn't delay myself any more.
After some time I arrived at the place,
I sat there patiently perched on my case.
Soon after that I walked away
Only to find that I'd got the wrong day!

Elysia Fawn (11)
St Peter's Catholic Primary School, Shoreham-by-Sea

Rainbow

Rainbow, rainbow, such an elegant thing,
What beautiful colours this creation will bring.
Red for anger, blazing in fire,
Spreading and growing higher and higher.
Orange for playing, symbolising fun,
While children are laughing and others run.
Yellow for happiness glowing with light,
Changing darkness into a wonderful sight.
Green for envy growing with ivy,
Twisting and turning, strangling tightly.
Blue is for the calm delicate sea,
When disturbed crashing silently.
Purple brings the deep sky to life,
As the moon pierces through like the sharpest knife.
Indigo, is the mystical one of them all,
Secrets hidden until they are called.
These individual colours come together and bind,
To miss this creation you'll be out of your mind.

Natalie Dalpadado (11)
St Peter's Catholic Primary School, Shoreham-by-Sea

Who Am I?

I am a big animal
I live in the sea
I change colour to hide from enemies
I have eight arms
You spot me in the bottom of the ocean
I am like a spider but I live in the water
I can be scary sometimes
What am I?

Ryan Bethune (11)
St Peter's Catholic Primary School, Shoreham-by-Sea

The Many Things That Can Happen To You While Reading A Book

1. You could get a paper cut, it could get infected and you'd get a serious disease.
2. The book could set alight, it could spread to you and you'd get burnt to death.
3. The ink could drip off, it could spill onto you, it could stain your clothes and then your mum will be so angry you'd be grounded for ten years.
4. The writing could be so small, it could make you dizzy and you'd go unconscious.
5. The book could be so heavy, you'd drop it and it could hit your head and you'd get a concussion.
6. You could read for so long, you'd get a migraine.
7. The book could be so disgusting, you'd be sick, and then you wouldn't go to school and miss the school residential trip.
8. While lying down the book could fall on your face and you'd suffocate.
9. The book could be so long; you'd fall asleep and miss your favourite programme on telly!
So actually I don't know why you're reading this book!

Joe McLoughlin (11)
St Peter's Catholic Primary School, Shoreham-by-Sea

Tuned Car

The first gear slams into action.
The exhaust roaring under power.
The engine pushing its revs to the limit.
The pedals getting pushed as far as they can go.
Nitro cooling the engine.
The brakes get slammed on.
Spinners on the wheels slow down as the car stops.

Jack Fry (11)
St Peter's Catholic Primary School, Shoreham-by-Sea

Don't

Don't put peas with cheese
Don't put pears with hairs
Don't put Mars Bars with Milky Stars

Don't put Sam with jam
Don't put Jack on your back
Don't put Josh with the Posh

Don't put red with your bed
Don't put green with the mean
Don't put yellow with a marshmallows

Don't take a look at a book
Don't lean on the Queen
Don't put tall with small

And definitely don't say don't to
Mr No Don'ts.

Toby Kelly (11)
St Peter's Catholic Primary School, Shoreham-by-Sea

Galloping Sea Horse

See galloping sea horses,
Prancing through the heavy tide.
Sea animals,
Floating in the water.
Big cute turtles,
Swimming above our heads.
Shoals of fish tickling fingers,
As they swim around.
We're floating on the sea.

James Topliff (11)
St Peter's Catholic Primary School, Shoreham-by-Sea

I Want To Be The Queen

I want to be the Queen.
So I could have lots and lots and lots of money,
And buy all the toys.
But then they would complain . . . but . . .
They can't blame the Queen!

I want to be the Queen.
So I can be taken around on a chariot and horses
And take up all the space on the road,
So I didn't have any traffic in front.
But then they would complain . . . but . . .
They can't blame the Queen!

I want to be the Queen.
So I could wear all the best clothes that dragged on the floor
So you have to clean all the floors in front
But everyone would complain . . . but . . .
They can't blame the Queen!

Actually I don't want to be the Queen,
Because the Queen causes trouble!

Joshua Jewiss (11)
St Peter's Catholic Primary School, Shoreham-by-Sea

SATs

Heart pounding as you wait for the test,
What will it be like? No one can guess.
Teachers trying to calm you down,
Trying to remember what's a noun?
Oh how we hate those *Silly Annoying Things!*
As quick as a flash it's all over,
Been revising since October.
But wait! You are forgetting,
That tomorrow we have to start all over again!
Oh how we hate those *Silly Annoying Things.*

Aisling Butler (11)
St Peter's Catholic Primary School, Shoreham-by-Sea

Cheese On Toast

Cheese on toast,
You smell the aroma,
It's so sensational,
Your nose twitches.

Cheese on toast,
You feel ecstatic when it's finished cooking,
The ooze of the cheese as you poke it,
You feel you want another one.

Cheese on toast,
You see inside your head
A cheese on toast on a silk, purple cushion,
You're bouncing on a giant yellow sun.

Cheese on toast,
You can hear the crunch of the toast,
The ooze of the cheese as it squeaks,
You hear the bubbling of the cheese as you bite into it.

Charlotte Anderson (11)
St Peter's Catholic Primary School, Shoreham-by-Sea

I Am A . . . Kennings

Body slamming
Arms jamming
Swift mover
Party groover
Silent hider
Fast briber
Crowd cheering
People fearing
Chips maker
People breaker
Never biter
Champion fighter!

Colin Colas (11)
St Peter's Catholic Primary School, Shoreham-by-Sea

Fire

Fire rushing, spreading, destroying, killing everything in its path.
Fire like guns, moving fast, shooting across the landscape,
Causing pain for anything that crosses its course.
Fire's anger, lively, out of control like an untamed wild beast.
The long living smell of the burning wood,
The stuffy heat is burning, staining onto our faces.
The sound of the crackling fire's flames.
After the wild fires die down,
The small little creatures start to emerge
From their fireproof homes and spread through the land,
Covering the black that was once green grass.

Callum Farrell (11)
St Peter's Catholic Primary School, Shoreham-by-Sea

Flowers

F is for flowers which shimmer in the sun.
L is for loveliness that sparkles in the light.
O is for oh how lovely.
W is for wonderland which brightens up the world.
E is for England the wonderful flowered garden.
R is for roses which shimmer in the sunlight.
S is for swaying flowers in the breeze.

Gemma Coyle (10)
St Peter's Catholic Primary School, Shoreham-by-Sea

What Am I?

I soar through the air
When I'm thrown or kicked.
In my game I sometimes am held
And people jump and catch me.
What am I?

A rugby ball.

Rhys Garrish (10)
St Peter's Catholic Primary School, Shoreham-by-Sea

The A To Z Of My Mum

A is for sure, absent-minded.
B she's quite beautiful.
C is for her caring job as a carer.
D is for a dear.
E quite elegant.
F is for forty-five!
G is nice and gentle.
H for always being happy.
I, very interesting.
J is for joyful.
K for kind.
L she's always lovely.
M for only my mummy.
N she loves doing needlework.
O quite original.
P she's pretty polite.
Q is for qualified.
R is for a great rainbow leader.
S is for a scenery lover.
T is trendy.
U she's a bit unusual.
V stands for VIP which means Very Important Person.
W for wonderful.
X she gives brilliant Xmas pressies
Y for yoghurt lover.
Z is definitely for z'best!

Anne Ballard (11)
St Peter's Catholic Primary School, Shoreham-by-Sea

Rocks

R ocks collect in caves.
O nly move when they are touched.
C arried by the waves.
K icked by shoes and not loved.
S o spare a thought for rocks.

Robyn James (11)
St Peter's Catholic Primary School, Shoreham-by-Sea

Thunder And Lightning

Thunder crashes
Lightning bashes
Buildings tumble
Floorboards rumble
Window smashes
Lightning dashes
But this is one side. It can be . . .

Daylight breaker
Underground shaker
Glass wounder
Is it all a rumour?

Sam Russell (11)
St Peter's Catholic Primary School, Shoreham-by-Sea

The Old Elephant

There was an old elephant who had big feet.
The problem was he wanted to eat.
He searched in the bushes but there was nothing there.
All he found were pieces of hair.
He looked up and down and searched all around.
But crushed leaves from his feet were all that he found.
His friends tried to tell him watch where you walk
But it was too late for them to talk.
There was an old elephant who had big feet.
The problem was he wanted to eat.

Katie Hart (11)
St Peter's Catholic Primary School, Shoreham-by-Sea

The Normal Teacher?

Nice smile,
Friendly face.
Good teacher,
Can play the bass.

But is this all completely true?
What is behind the façade she shows?
Only one way to know.

I followed her home late that night
When I received a terrible fright.
She peeled off her disguise and the ugly mask
To reveal a face which left me aghast.

Red eyes, green face
Long nose, warts like a mace
I almost fell out of the tree
With the horror she gave me.
Now I had a photo of her face
I knew her past, I could trace.

The next day at school I knew what to do,
I showed my friends the proof in the loo.
We all agreed, as well as beauty she lacked,
She needed to go and never come back.

We told our teacher about what we knew
And she agreed to get out of the school.
We saw her spaceship,
And like an eagle up it flew.

So is your teacher much like this?
Who knows? But remember this advice.
Though your teacher may jump with bliss
She could be an alien in her real life.

Nageswaran Kalidasan (11)
St Peter's Catholic Primary School, Shoreham-by-Sea

Weather

When the weather is hot
The sky is clear and blue
You can plant a flower in a pot
And let the sun shine on you.

When the weather is wet
The sky is dull and grey
The children run out to get their pet
The birds will not come to play.

When the weather is snowing
The sky is white and full
The children will be throwing
Their giant snowball.

When the weather is foggy
You cannot see the sky
The ground is very soggy
And now we say goodbye.

Rachael Smith (10)
Singlewell CP School, Gravesend

The Hunter

I'm a mighty hunter
Lying in the bush.

I'm a mighty hunter
Everybody shush!

I'm a mighty hunter
I see buffalo run.

I'm a mighty hunter
Bang! goes my gun.

Billy Luker (8)
Singlewell CP School, Gravesend

My Cats

I have two cats,
One's thin, one's fat
One's called Pickle
He likes a tickle
One's called Lillie
And she's really silly.

Lillie is black,
With a soft back.
Pickle is fluffy,
And very scruffy
I love my cats very much
They are soft to touch.

Pickle and Lillie are my pals
And when they purr they sound like owls.
They like to play everyday,
And I want them to stay with me forever!

Anne-Marie Wilson (7)
Singlewell CP School, Gravesend

Football

The sun is out let's have some fun,
Football's good for everyone.
Up and down the pitch we go,
Hooray, hooray, we've scored a goal.
We jump and shout and celebrate,
That brings our score up to eight.
The other boys are tired and sad,
We are happy and really glad.
The whistle blows,
The game is over.
We've won again,
Up and up the league we go,
To the top,
Let's hope so!

Sam Goddard (7)
Singlewell CP School, Gravesend

I Love Pets

Everybody likes cats
Then I'll chat to the cat

Everybody likes dogs
Then I'll draw a picture of a dog

Everybody likes rabbits
Then the rabbit will rap to the tap

Everybody likes puppies
Then I'll paint a picture of the puppy.

Heidi Gaskin (8)
Singlewell CP School, Gravesend

Pets

Cats are cute because they have soft fur
Cats are cuddly and they purr.

Dogs are great, big and small
Some are short and some are tall.
Some are tame
Some are scary.
Some are smart
And some are hairy!

Francesca Bonfield (8)
Singlewell CP School, Gravesend

Cats

Cats are kind and cute when you comfort them
They will comfort you when you are sad and lonely

They love milk and pieces of string
Sometimes they sound like hoovers when they purr so loudly.

Cats are very lovely but they can be vicious sometimes.

Amber Hollins (8)
Singlewell CP School, Gravesend

Make-Up Day

Make-up day is so so gay
Waiting at the make-up shop
Trying to pay for my stock.

Now for dressing up.
I go downtown to buy a gown
I chose a pretty pink then I start to think
To buy a matching hat
I change my mind and pick a tiara because it is fairer.

Now for my earrings.
Should I choose the studs, the big earrings or the dangly ones?
The studs are no fun, I pick some big ones.

Now for my hair.
How about a bun or some curls?
The curls my friend with beads like pearls on the ends.

Now for home.
I brush my teeth and floss then I put on some lip gloss
Finally I put on mascara and some blusher.

Now for the disco . . .

Claire Morris (7)
Singlewell CP School, Gravesend

Friends

My best friend is Anne-Marie.
She is always good company.
We run, jump, skip and play.
It is best if it is a sunny day.
I like it when she comes for tea.
She makes me laugh when she tickles me.
We jump on the trampoline so high.
We are trying hard to reach the sky.
We have fun and do lots together.
I hope we will be friends forever and ever.

Megan Ayley (7)
Singlewell CP School, Gravesend

The Three Little Pigs

Once upon a time far, far away,
Three little pigs went on a holiday.
'Let's go to Africa, no, India,' the smallest pig said,
But their mum decided they'd go to New York instead.
So they packed their bags and off they went,
They travelled by car from Gravesend, Kent.
On the journey a wolf came by,
He said his name was Shirley but they knew it was a lie.
They arrived at New York five years later,
They went in a restaurant and saw a hairy waiter.
She looked very strange but definitely not pale
She had googly eyes and a very bushy tail.
'It's the wolf, it's the wolf, it's the wolf,' they cried,
'Quickly let's get outside!'
'Come here, come here, come here little pigs,'
Said the wolf with a grin.
'Not for the hairs on my chinny chin chin!'
They went back home and never left again!

Jessica Hunt (8)
Singlewell CP School, Gravesend

Hamsters

Some hamsters are big
Some hamsters are small
They're so cuddly and some aren't at all.
And when they wake they can feel okay
They twitch their nose
And go to sleep in their bed.
Hamsters like to play in their ball
And eat their snack all day long.
Some hamsters look cute.
Some look kind.
They do what they want to do in their cage all the time.
I wish my hamster stayed in my room.
My hamster is the best in the world.

Nicola Thompson (7)
Singlewell CP School, Gravesend

I Love Pets

I love pets, they're great fun,
I love pets and I have one.
My pet's a hamster called Tiny.

I love pets, they're great fun,
I love pets and I have one
A rabbit called Greg,
He's grey, white and brown.

He's not very nice at all
The hamster is inside, the rabbit is out.
I love pets.
They're great fun!

Chantay White (8)
Singlewell CP School, Gravesend

Toffee

I have a rabbit called Toffee.
I love her very much.
We play together and never stop.
I will love her as long as I live.
So, never take Toffee away from me!
She lives in a cage downstairs and munches on food!
I will love her as long as I live.

Charlotte Brown (7)
Singlewell CP School, Gravesend

Squeeze

We love to *squeeze* bananas,
We love to *squeeze* ripe plums,
And when we are feeling sad
We love to *squeeze* our mums.

Hannah Cox (8)
Singlewell CP School, Gravesend

Fast Car!

The car goes zooming down the highway
The engine roaring
Its neon lights are bright
The hydraulics make it bounce up and down
The stereo blasting, it feels all alone in the night
Then another car, speeding behind its lights are flashing
Oh no! You're busted!
Stop! Police!

Jamie Gilbert (8)
Singlewell CP School, Gravesend

Brownies

B rownies is great
R unning around
O ut and about
W earing uniform if you've got on
N ever leaving a Brownie out
 I nteresting things to do
E veryone is friendly
S ing Brownie songs.

Chloe Kitchen (7)
Singlewell CP School, Gravesend

Colours Of The Rainbow

Red for roses
Orange for marigolds
Yellow for daffodils
Green for grass
Blue for bluebells
Violet for violets
Indigo for lavender
All these colours are here for you and I to see
On the ground and in the sky.

Callum Cherrison (8)
Singlewell CP School, Gravesend

The Monster In The Cupboard

The monster in the cupboard is very scary.
He's fat, round, short and hairy.
He has sharp teeth and filthy ears.
His claws dig in as hard as spears.
When I am skipping,
The monster tries and he keeps tripping.
Once when it was raining I made him some clothes,
But goodness knows what happened to those!
I took the monster in my tree house, there he got trapped.
The tree house suddenly snapped.
I played hide-and-seek, me and the monster too.
I pretended I didn't know where he was, but all along I knew.
We went out on the climbing frame
The monster used his feet which worked just the same.
We went outside and climbed the tree
He went as quick as lightning you see.
When I pushed him down the hill on a sledge
He made a hole right through the hedge.
The best thing is he's my friend
I'm sad to say this is the end.

Bethany Chuter (9)
Singlewell CP School, Gravesend

The Writer Of This Poem

(Based on 'The Writer of this Poem' by Roger McGough)

The writer of this poem
Is as gentle as a lamb,
As pretty as a garden,
As daring as most others,
And is braver than you!

The writer of this poem
Is as clever as a book,
As brown as brunettes
As clean as a mother
And is sharper than a nib.

Megan Salter (9)
Singlewell CP School, Gravesend

My Horse Called Honey

I have a horse called Honey
She is extremely funny
She gallops round the field like a crazy act
And when I ride her she's a maniac.
She sings on the karaoke
Her favourite is Elvis Presley
I put her in a race
She came last at a very slow pace
In her hair she wears a red bow
And wears it well with a radiant glow
She loves to go ice skating
And is brilliant at cake making
My horse Honey
Is as cuddly as a bunny
At night she cuddles up to me
And we both drink tea.
I love my horse Honey.

Holly Hewitt (9)
Singlewell CP School, Gravesend

My Pet Rabbit

I have a fabulous rabbit
Who is as black as black can be,
He has long floppy ears which reach to his toes,
Big, brown eyes and a rather wet nose.
He likes to eat carrots, apples and hay,
Spring greens and broccoli, I give him each day.
He lives in a hutch that my dad put together,
It has an upstairs and downstairs and is out in all weather.
With a plastic cover that keeps out the rain,
Mum cleans him out again and again.
His name is Sooty and he is so sweet
My neighbours say he looks good enough to eat!

Kelly Gardiner (8)
Singlewell CP School, Gravesend

Foxendown Pony Sanctuary

Ponies saved from slaughter and torture.
Tall ones, small ones,
Fat ones, thin ones,
They all come to Foxendown.
There's Bobby and Solly,
Ellie and Bella,
Tara and Amber
To say just a few.
They are all loved by Pat
Their saviour from Hell to Heaven.
Pat cares for them all
We children love them,
We ride them and feed them
Brush and clean them.
Thomas, Lass, Star, Angel and Rabbit
We love and care for them all.

Heather Robertson (9)
Singlewell CP School, Gravesend

I Love Pets

Some are fluffy
Some are puffy
Puppies are cute and loyal
And if I had one
I would call it Tuffy.

Cats are hairy,
Witches' cats are scary.
Rabbits are fast
I don't think if I raced mine
I would ever cross the finish line.

Fish are boring
You can't play with them
If I had one I could call it Pen or Ken.

Rebecca Johnson (8)
Singlewell CP School, Gravesend

Poem
(Based on 'The Writer of this Poem' by Roger McGough)

The writer of this poem is as strong as a rhino
Is as quick as a cheetah
Is as tall as a tree
Is as clever as a teacher.

Is as sly as a cat
Is as playful as a dog
Is as black as a bat.

Is as hungry as a pig
Is as cheeky as a monkey
Is as fragile as a twig
The writer of this poem tells lies.

Luke Thompson (9)
Singlewell CP School, Gravesend

Aliens On The Bus

Aliens on the bus,
Whatever bus they go on
They make a big fuss!

Some like to sing,
Some like trying on rings
Some are spotty,
Some are dotty.

Now on the bus some are juggling
Spotty Jake is speaking
And Laughing Sam is eating.

Aliens on the bus!

Callum Howes (8)
Singlewell CP School, Gravesend

Mike And Spike

There once was a boy called Mike
Who had a dog called Spike,
Spike was on a diet
But he would not be quiet,
Mike bought Spike some special dog food for dinner
But Spike did not get any thinner,
Mike wonders and wonders what to do
Because Spike spends all day on the loo!
Mike takes Spike to the vet,
In the end Mike has to buy a new pet,
He doesn't know why, but no one does yet,
Not even the assistant vet.

Patrick Mitchell (9)
Singlewell CP School, Gravesend

Skateboarder

Skateboarder, skateboarder speeding by
Slalom, halfpipe, spin in the sky
Skateboarder, skateboarder wheels all spinning
Push once more and he's nearly winning
From side to side he rides the pipe
Twisting, turning as he makes the height
Skateboarder, skateboarder speeding by
Slalom, halfpipe, spin in the sky
Ollie, kick flip, 360 turn
Super twist and there's more to burn
Trucks are sparking grinding the rail
The crowd all cheering hoping he won't fail
Skateboarder, skateboarder, one more bend
Hip hip hooray, he's at the end!

Lewis Wade (9)
Singlewell CP School, Gravesend

Football, Football

The teams are in place
All ready to go
We all wait the referee's whistle to blow.

The ball is passed from player to player
Tackling, dribbling, chipping the ball
Run past the defender he's way too tall.

He's nearly there, the goal post's in sight
One more kick with all his might
Just the goalie to beat, it's a sure bet
He kicks the ball
Yes it's in the net.

The teams are in place
All ready to go
We all wait the referee's whistle to blow.

Jack Wade (9)
Singlewell CP School, Gravesend

Peanut My Dog

Peanut is my dog
She is small and white and fluffy,
She sleeps with me,
She licks my feet,
She snuggles up to me,
She is my mate.

I love my little Peanut,
She nibbles things she shouldn't
Although she is a pest,
She barks at everything she sees
But I will always love my Peanut,
She is my special dog.

James Bell (9)
Singlewell CP School, Gravesend

Oooh-Arrgh-Ha-Ha-Hah

Oooh-arrgh-ha-ha-hah!
That's my evil laugh.
It sounds best when it echoes
So I practise in the bath.

Oooh-arrgh-ha-ha-hah!
There I go again,
I sometimes even scare myself
Every now and then.

Oooh-arrgh-ha-ha-hah
Why don't you join in?
Bare your teeth and squint your eyes
Now with an evil grin.

Oooh-arrgh-ha-ha-hah
What a wicked grin!

Rachael Cox (10)
Singlewell CP School, Gravesend

I Met A Boy From Earth

I met a boy from Earth
Who said, 'I don't know how to surf'
He was on a journey
To find out about Lenny Herky
Lenny Herky was a bloke
And he always used to smoke
Then he turned into a folk
He always used to mope.
And always used to wash himself with soap
The boy said, 'I know how to surf'
Now that's the boy from Earth.

Jessica Hutton (10)
Singlewell CP School, Gravesend

In The Morning

'Wake up, wake up you're going to be late,
Yesterday when the bell went you were still at the school gate!'
'Coming, coming I'm making my bed!'
'Well leave that until later, have your breakfast instead!'
'But I can't find my bowl and the bread's all gone,
Where am I supposed to get any more from?'
'Never mind that, just get yourself dressed,
Your face is all dirty and your hair's a mess!'
'I can't find the toothpaste, the soap's all over the place,
I need a flannel or I can't wash my face!'
'Are you ready yet?'
'Nearly, I'm just about set!
Just looking for my school skirt, where is it?'
'I don't know, look around a bit!'
'OK, I'm dressed just packing my rucksack!'
'Don't forget your lunch, put that in your pack!'
'No I won't I'm getting my book!'
'Hurry up, hurry up have a quick look!'
'Yes I've got it, I'm coming down to you!'
'Just get to school on time, whatever you do.'
'Right at last, I think I'm ready to go, hold on, stop!'
'Oh, what now, you haven't forgotten your top?'
'No . . . but . . . it's Saturday!'

Natalie Hickmott (11)
Singlewell CP School, Gravesend

Playground Bullies

Playground bullies are not very good
They upset children in the neighbourhood
Kids tell the teachers and they sort it out
Stop them bullies! We want them out!
Kids should be safe in their neighbourhood
Let's get together and make sure we're understood!

Charley Whyte (9)
Singlewell CP School, Gravesend

Sports

Football is played on a field and
Sometimes the goalkeeper uses the defenders as a shield.
Rugby is a rough sport,
The idea is not to get caught.
In badminton you have to hit a shuttle
But don't be too subtle.
The games I hate are polo and squash
They are only played by people who are posh.
Three wooden stumps is a wicket
A wicket is used in cricket.
Ball and racket that's tennis
And sometimes it's played in Venice.
A stick and a ball that's hockey
The ball is really hard and hurts, so don't get cocky!

Josh Law   (11)
Singlewell CP School, Gravesend

As Swift As A Swallow

As swift as a swallow
As sluggish as a snail.

As high as a cloud
As low as the ground.

As sticky as toffee
As smooth as coffee.

As prickly as a hedgehog
As cuddly as my toy dog.

As buzzy as a bee
As cheery as a chimpanzee.

As long as time
As short as this rhyme.

Amy Rolfe (9)
Singlewell CP School, Gravesend

The Pony

I ride horses at Knight Place Farm,
The horses here won't do any harm,
If you go up there, it's in Stroud,
The people there aren't at all rude.

There's Kyra, Smarty, Donnie and more,
All in a row behind their door,
Washed, brushed and cleaned and ready for you
Waiting to show you what they can do.

My favourite horse there is called Roly,
He trots and canters very slowly,
My teacher, Laura, teaches us everything she knows,
Jumping, cantering and dressage shows.

I rode Roly, Hannah rode Bart
He was standing there ready to start,
Georgina rode Monty, Mum was there too,
Watching and smiling at what we could do.

So if you want lessons to learn how to ride,
Give Card a ring, she'll be your guide,
My name is Alice I ride at one
See you there and we'll have some fun!

Alice Ellison (10)
Singlewell CP School, Gravesend

Butterflies

Dance on the flowers they flip and flap about
Butterflies are nice
Butterflies are colourful
Butterflies are pretty.

Butterflies if you go and touch them
Will shrivel and die
And suddenly they're on the floor
All flat and still.

Sarah Lane (10)
Singlewell CP School, Gravesend

My Dream

I want a puppy,
It could be chubby.
I'd want to play all day,
But if it was tired, it would be okay.

No matter about my hobby,
Or my boyfriend Bobby.
My friends could come to visit,
Everyone would want to kiss it.

It would be big and bouncy,
Its hair long and flouncy.
It would scare away strangers,
And look after babies in mangers.

It would be all mine,
Everything would be absolutely fine.

Hollie Mason (11)
Singlewell CP School, Gravesend

Kitten Cat

Black cat all nice and silky,
Likes to drink tea, nice and milky,
Have you got any lies
Within your eyes?

No matter whether plump or thin cats,
They always like to lie on a mat,
The size doesn't matter,
They might grow fatter.

Whether small or sweet,
Everyone would like to meet,
They might be alone,
But they will still get back home.

Rachael Hurcombe (10)
Singlewell CP School, Gravesend

School, School, School

My name is Tony and I like my school,
In the mornings we meet in the hall,
To listen to the teachers setting out the day,
But all we really want is to play.

My teacher's name is Mrs Green,
Although sometimes she is very mean,
She arrives at school every day
To teach us how to learn and play.

She teaches us very much, we would be lost to see her leave,
But without us I am sure she would be sad,
Sometimes we can be very bad.

When I come home from school I can relax and be cool,
Because the next day I have to return to school,
Once I relax and be cool and finally I can play with my football.

Tony Lambert (10)
Singlewell CP School, Gravesend

My Guinea Pig

I used to have a guinea pig
Who ran around all day.
I used to give him lots of cucumber
To help him on his way.
He used to eat lots of grass and dandelions too.
I miss my little guinea pig I really, really do.

I used to give him a brush and a groom
He did not like it though.
I used to like to cuddle him and never let him go.
I love my little guinea pig I really miss him so.

Elisha Waghorn (10)
Singlewell CP School, Gravesend

The Stallion

His galloping hooves thunder across the plain,
As the howling wind calls his name,
He flicks his mane and swishes his tail,
As he makes his journey through the gusty gale.

His piebald coat keeps his strong body warm,
As he fights his way through the terrible storm,
His neighs echo throughout the night,
And his big brown eyes are wide in fright.

The plain is replaced by woodland trees,
As the terrible storm begins to cease,
Nothing is stirring, not a single bird,
For he's found his way back to his herd.

Emily Liquorish (11)
Singlewell CP School, Gravesend

Gym

On a Friday night
I go through the door into the gym,
I move my head up and down,
I move my chin round and round,
I move my arms as I spin,
I go up into a bridge as the coaches tell me.

I go on bars,
I go on floor,
I run up the vault track,
I walk on the white line
To the trampoline and sit down as my coach tells me.
When it finishes I am exhausted!

Ria Gwalter (10)
Singlewell CP School, Gravesend

My Love

Sometimes I wake up crying.
Sometimes I feel like dying.
But you're the only one that keeps me alive.

I think about you night and day.
You're the only one that makes me stay.
I love you so it hurts to see you go.

I think you're great I would hate to hate but
I think you're absolutely marvellous.

Rory Newman (11)
Singlewell CP School, Gravesend

Dogs

A dog can be black; a dog can be white,
Some dogs aren't vicious but others will bite,
Some dogs are big, others are small,
Some are so lazy they do nothing at all.

A dog can be stern or like to play,
A dog can be grumpy or be very gay,
Some dogs are very good, some dogs are bad,
Some dogs are happy while others are sad.

Ian Thompson (10)
Singlewell CP School, Gravesend

The Rainbow

The rainbow is colourful.
The rainbow is wide.
The rainbow is arch shaped.
Let's have a look inside . . .
It's red, orange and yellow,
With green, blue and indigo,
And not forgetting violet.

Anna Rolfe (10)
Singlewell CP School, Gravesend

My Cat Is A Detective

My cat is a detective.
She is great at solving clues.
She once caught me in the fridge drinking my dad's booze.

My cat is a detective.
She is great at solving clues.
She even saw my baby brother rapping to the blues.

My cat is a detective.
She is great at finding clues.
She even saw my sister trying on my mum's new shoes.

Jack Baldwin (10)
Singlewell CP School, Gravesend

A Crazy Poem

Little Bo Peep lost her sheep
She went up the hill and found a pill
And then she fell in love with a dove.

Who loved her too but had a coo
On her head in a shed.
Then it flew in the air, knocked down a pair,
That fell on the floor and vibrated the door,
So the kids couldn't play anymore.

James Flaherty (10)
Singlewell CP School, Gravesend

Butterfly

Beautiful butterfly,
Fluttering prettily,
Alighting on petals with powdery wings
Fragile and frail,
Perfectly painted
What delicate life to the garden she brings.

Lucy Hickmott (10)
Singlewell CP School, Gravesend

The Life Of A Sunflower

I am lonely under the silent dark soil,
Damp and cold,
But suddenly I emerge from my deep, dark hiding place,
I can see rays of light shining down on me keeping me warm,
I am all alone but I am first to see the outdoors,
First to see the sun,
First to see our new home,
First to see the world.

The April showers begin to fall, the sun begins to shine,
I feel alive I stretch my stem and leaves,
I sway in the summer breeze,
The ladybird flies onto my petals,
The spider spins its delicate lace,
Web of silk,
The butterfly flutters by,
But now the air feels chilly.

I have been forgotten,
Watered less every day,
Covered by gold and red leaves,
I am beginning to die,
My petals start to lose colour,
Fading,
I suddenly begin to grow cold,
Freezing,
I have no life at all,
I bow and fall.

Bethany Sibun (11)
Singlewell CP School, Gravesend

The Old Man From Mocket

There was a man from Mocket
He took a ride in a rocket
The rocket went bang
His beeb went clang
And found his beeb in his pocket.

Ben May (10)
Singlewell CP School, Gravesend

Summer

Flowers sway in the summer breeze,
All of our shorts just touch our knees.

Everyone knows when the fun has begun,
It's when you shine, beautiful sun.

Head to the seaside, touch the sand
Feel the smoothness run through your hand.

Let's all go to the deep blue sea
Come on then, you and me.

Do you love the summer sun?
It's when the boring things turn to fun.

Yucky sand in our tea
Look at everyone playing happily.

Shells and stones
And yummy ice cream cones.

Hannah Toulson (9)
Singlewell CP School, Gravesend

I Love My Little Pony

I love my little pony,
She trots around all day,
She canters with a neigh
And hopes to play again.

I love my little pony,
With a grey and white mane,
I ride her in the sunshine,
And I ride her in the rain,
Then she wants to play again.

I love my little pony,
At the end of the day,
She eats all the hay,
And has a little lay,
Then asks to play again.

Hayley Rolf (10)
Singlewell CP School, Gravesend

Apples!

Apples are red,
Rosy and round
When they are ripe,
They fall to the ground.
Some are sour, some are sweet,
Some are juicy and lovely to eat.

Some are used in cooking and drinks,
Some for pies and puddings I think,
Some of those fell to the ground,
Are put in a box when the horses come round.

Jodie Gibbs (10)
Singlewell CP School, Gravesend

Cricket

He holds the ball, red and shiny,
Runs up to bowl, getting faster,
Throws the ball with his arm out straight,
It bounces once and *whack!*
Ball goes into the sky higher, higher,
Down it comes lower, lower,
Two hands come out ready to catch,
And in it goes - *howzat!*

Andrew Windsor (10)
Singlewell CP School, Gravesend

My Trampoline

My trampoline is big and wide
It springs like it's never done before
When I jump I feel like I'm flying
When I hit the ground I spring back up
It feels like you're on your own springs
And I feel like I have wings.

Daniella Bates (11)
Singlewell CP School, Gravesend

Gran Can You Rap?

Granny came for tea one day
I was bored and wanted to play.
I asked her if she could rap
She held up her hands and started to clap.
She began to move like she didn't care,
She jumped up and down and shook her hair.
She sat back down; I think she needed a nap,
I think my granny is the Queen of Rap.

Mitchell Dossetter (10)
Singlewell CP School, Gravesend

Family Poem

There was a man called Pat
Who had a great big fat cat.
There was a lady called Val
Who had a great big fat tail.
There was a boy called Ben
Who had a great big den.
There was a girl called Pam
Who kept eating jam.

Emma Leaver (9)
Singlewell CP School, Gravesend

Horses

Horses are colour blind,
And practically kind.
All of them bite and are very, very bad.
I go very *mad,*
I love horses,
Mine goes on courses!
I love horses!

Hannah Ellison (9)
Singlewell CP School, Gravesend

Spring Surprises

Flowers are appearing everywhere,
Beautiful colours, cheery, vibrant,
Exciting smells, from sunflowers
To sweet smelling roses.
What could it be? It's the spring surprise!

Lambs are bleating in every field,
Sheeps' woolly fleeces are being shorn,
New lambs are being born everywhere,
Lambs and sheep leaping and grazing in the field,
What could it be? It's the spring surprise!

Hear the children talking so loud,
Singing and dancing all in a ring,
The animals being petted while they graze,
Can you smell the fresh spring air?
What could it be? It's the spring surprise!

Can you see, the streets are crowded,
People are noisy, children wandering in the streets,
The parks are busy, the shops are crowded,
The animals enjoy their new life,
What could it be? It's the spring surprise!

Lauren Ludlow (10)
Singlewell CP School, Gravesend

My Church At The Bottom Of The Hill

My favourite place across the park and down the hill,
Is a church so beautiful and peaceful.
I go there every day to show my thanks to God
I study the stained-glass window
Which tell the wonderful stories!
I shall always go to my church and never stay away
I shall always sing and pray.
I love my church at the bottom of the hill.

Hollie Courtney (10)
Singlewell CP School, Gravesend

The Dog

The dog was very cunning,
And his coat was all stunning,
His owner was cruel,
And he ate some mule.

The dog was all clumsy,
After being called dumbsy.
He steadily walked and fell in a pool,
Then a boy threw a ball in the pool.

He vigorously gulped it,
Just like a little bulb appeared in front of him.
He started feeling unwell,
Just as if his head was stuck down a well.

He wandered around the pool,
Until he collapsed in a fall.
He was rushed to a hospital,
And they took out the ball.
So he was happy
I'm glad he is cheerful.

Aaron Alderson (10)
Singlewell CP School, Gravesend

Football

F ootball fans eagerly wait queuing outside the stadium gates
O utbursts of songs echo around the grounds the
O pposition are also around
T ickets clutched in our hands, making our way to the
football stands
B oots bang against the ball, the other team are heading for a fall
A t full-time the whistle blows the home teams faces begin to glow
L oudly we cheer the game is won
L ong live Tottenham our number one!

Kamuran Gullu (10)
Singlewell CP School, Gravesend

Mystery Monster

You wake with a start
In the dead of the night
Your toes all exposed
And your blanket pulled up tight.

What was that noise?
What was that thump?
Was there something in the corner,
That was going bump?

The shadows are getting
Oh, so very near.
You cannot move because
You're filled with dread and fear.

Then you see something
By the window sill
It's a hand reaching out
Waiting to kill.

Your knees are knocking
Your teeth are chattering.
You're sweaty and horrid
It's not very flattering.

The thing's moving closer
It's under your bed.
You want to look
But you can't move your head.

It's getting ready to grab you
You're paralysed with fear.
You scream and you shout
And grab something near.

Then the light flickers on
Your mum's there, it's not as it seems.
She hugs you and tells you
It's all in your dreams.

She tucks you in tight
Back into bed.
She tells you not to worry
It's all in your head.

You hope for the best
And start counting sheep.
It won't be long till you're
Back to sleep.

This time I hope
My dream will be sweet.
And instead of a nightmare
It will be a treat.

Lewis Hudson (9)
Slade Green Junior School, Erith

I Was Going On A Journey

I was going on a journey to the afterlife
And I sprinted down the creepy, crawly, creaky path.
Then I saw a ginormous pile of gloopy, gloop
Then I kept skating down the horrid path.
Suddenly I saw a very dangerous creature
It had two ginormous pointy ears and eight wobbly legs.
Later we saw lovely flowers.
Suddenly it started to lash its sword at me.
However, I crawled past it.
Next I actually saw a musical skeleton; it wasn't bad it was good.
So I kept skipping along during my journey.
I saw a sleeping guardian and crept past him.
I saw a nasty creature, it floated up to me.
Suddenly I saw a green, purple, black, blue cow, I kept walking.
Suddenly I heard a noise behind me on the bus,
It was a small mouse.
It was going on a journey.

Christien Ives (9)
The Oaks Primary School, Crawley

Line Up

It's lunchtime everyone's here
Y3, Y4, Y5, Y6 line up
Off we go to get our food
Quietly wait line up

Tell them what you want
Then say, 'Thank you'
Move along the line
Get pudding then say, 'Thank you'

All finished outside to play
Rushing around hot and red
Tired and worn out
Need a drink hot and red

When the bell goes
Y3, Y4, Y5, Y6 all line up
Pushing and shoving
'Will you all line up?'

Luke Bailey (10)
The Ridgeway Primary School, Reading

Party Party

Party party
We've got to make
Party party
A birthday cake.

Party party
Blow up balloons
Party party
Playing the tunes.

Party party
Pass the parcel
Party party
Bouncy castle.

Dana Lee (10)
The Ridgeway Primary School, Reading

The King Of Quizzical Island

(Based on 'The King of Quizzical Island' by Gordon Snell)

The King of Quizzical Island
Had a most inquisitive mind.
He said, 'If I sail to the edge of the world
I wonder what I'll find?'

So he sailed on a turtle that took him to Mars
He found himself with zombies eating motorbike riders
Dinosaurs playing noughts and crosses, marshmallows playing tennis
Chickens riding scramblers, rabbits chasing tigers.

So the King eats cookies with the zombies,
Plays noughts and crosses with the dinosaurs,
Plays tennis with the marshmallows,
Rides scramblers with the chickens
And chases the tigers with the rabbits.

When he got back to his kingdom
He sorted things out for his next journey.
For his journey he's going to go to a motorway
Where there is mayhem.

Travis Fisher (9)
The Ridgeway Primary School, Reading

School Dinners

Icky dinners
Micky's dinners
Nasty little sickly dinners
Chicken dinners which are Nicky's dinners
Icky dinners turn to sticky dinners
Micky's dinners turn to Ricky's dinner
Nicky's dinners are kicky dinners
Nasty little sicky dinners turn to the best
Dinners which are *school dinners!*

Ryan Wakeford (9)
The Ridgeway Primary School, Reading

What Is Gold?

What is gold?
A ring is gold shining in the cold.

What is blue?
A dolphin is blue jumping up in front of the big ship's crew.

What is yellow?
Amber is yellow on the farmer's bed where people say hello.

What is grey?
Clouds are grey raining all day.

What is red?
Roses are red in their posh bed.

What is black?
A killer whale is black that has just hit someone on the back.

What is silver?
A star is silver reflecting in the river.

Stephen Byrnes (8)
The Ridgeway Primary School, Reading

What Is Green?

What is green?
The grass is green with flowers in-between.

What is gold?
A medal is gold as it shines in the light.

What is black?
Shoes are black that you polish with a brush.

What is red?
Poppies are red in the grass.

What is orange?
An orange just an orange.

Jordan Hathaway (8)
The Ridgeway Primary School, Reading

Longleat Safari Park Monkeys

There are monkeys cute,
Monkeys old
Monkeys friendly
And they all eat fruit.

They jump all over cars
Such naughty monkeys
They live free from bars.

Some pull the exhaust pipe off the back
Some are ginger
Some are striped
And some are grey and black.

Some are brown
Some make dents
Some are up trees
And some are down.

Their climbing's very good
Some are very silly
Some are very funny
They jump over wood.

Some are very geeky
So you had better
Watch out!
They are all very cheeky.

Sherri Martin (10)
The Ridgeway Primary School, Reading

You!

You! Your arms are like bottles.
You! Your eyes are like marbles.
You! Your nostrils are like beans.
You! Your head is like an egg.
You! Your belly is like a swollen blackboard.

Ashley Waters (8)
The Ridgeway Primary School, Reading

Ten Little Children

(Inspired by 'Ten Little Schoolboys' by A A Milne)

Ten little children
Standing in a line
One fell over
Then there were nine.

Nine little children
Who were very late
One fell down and cut herself
Then there were eight.

Eight little children
Going to Heaven
One fell down
And then there were seven.

Seven little children
Were balancing on bricks
One fell down
And then there were six.

Six little children
Looked at a hive
One got stung
And then there were five.

Sarah Savid (8)
The Ridgeway Primary School, Reading

Christmas Means . . .

Christmas means . . .
Snow flowing over the trees
Reindeers in the sky with sparkling eyes
Christmas carols and children singing
Sparkling lights oh so bright
They look at night.

Andy Makepiece (8)
The Ridgeway Primary School, Reading

You!

You!
Your bed is like a dinosaur.

You!
Your ears are like an elephants.

You!
Your eyes are like jelly eyes.

You!
Your belly is like a big blackboard.

You!
Your leg is like a brick.

You!
Your backside is like a hut.

You!
Your nostril is like a donut.

Lewis Bailey (8)
The Ridgeway Primary School, Reading

What Is Yellow?

What is yellow?
The sun is yellow shining in the sky.

What is green?
The grass is green blowing in the wind.

What is green?
The leaves are green flying in the wind.

What is blue?
The sky is blue as blue as the sea.

What is gold?
A ring is gold and shiny like the sun.

Michael Gonzalez (8)
The Ridgeway Primary School, Reading

The King Of Quizzical Island

(Based on 'The King of Quizzical Island' by Gordon Snell)

The King of Quizzical Island
Had a most inquisitive mind.
He said, 'If I sail to the edge of the world
I wonder what I'll find?'

So he sailed in a chocolate boat
He saw a drum fish
And was chased by a goat
And had a big wish.

He found himself on Incredible Island
The dinosaurs were drinking coffee
And fish riding a motorbike
He had a toffee.

He went to the disco with the dogs
He went to Popcorn Mountain.
He had coffee with the dinosaurs
And had a drink at the fountain.

He went back in a chocolate boat
Looked at the clouds which were made of glass.
He turned in the road and then
He was lost!

Kensley Maloney (9)
The Ridgeway Primary School, Reading

You!

You! Your head is like a football.
You! Your eyes are like jelly beans.
You! Your ears are like tomatoes.
You! Your arms are like sticks.
You! Your feet are like bananas.
You! Your fingers are like sausages.
You! Your legs are like tree stumps.

Chelsea Ivell (8)
The Ridgeway Primary School, Reading

The King Of Quizzical Island

(Based on 'The King of Quizzical Island' by Gordon Snell)

The King of Quizzical Island
Had a most inquisitive mind.
He said, 'If I sail to the edge of the world
I wonder what I will find?'

So he sailed along the ocean
On a flying saucer spoon
And as he was travelling
He saw a magic moon.

When he got to Chewy Island
He saw a magic wing.
It had green and yellow feathers
And it gave a massive ding.

He was tired
So he went to sleep
He woke up in the morning
And gave a little peep.

He went across the ocean
Eating everything he saw
After he ate that
He wanted some more!

Kyle Trotman (9)
The Ridgeway Primary School, Reading

About My Funny Monkey Lee

Lee, Lee the monkey is so funny and so cheeky
With his big teeth and curly tail and his tiny brown ears.
Lee, Lee the monkey is so nice and so playful
With a banana in one hand and a cheeky grin he is so nice to me.

Marie McHugh (10)
The Ridgeway Primary School, Reading

The King Of Quizzical Island

(Based on 'The King of Quizzical Island' by Gordon Snell)

The King of Quizzical Island
Had a most inquisitive mind.
He said, 'If I sail to the edge of the river
I wonder what I'll find?'

He saw a purple sparkling mountain and a jumping tree
He passed a strange island with gold painting down the side.
And he saw the tree munching trees
Funny or not, he couldn't decide.

He went to meet the munching trees
And the trees who could take the gold.
But you have to look after it
The King said, 'The gold is cold.'

The King said, 'It's very, very fun being rich'
Then trees came to take the gold back.
The King said, 'Please don't take it back,
We have to put it back in the sack.'

Dan Muchui (8)
The Ridgeway Primary School, Reading

Beach

When you see the sea what do you see?
I see waves crashing, bouncing up high.

When you see the golden sand what do you see?
I see the golden sand blazing in the sun watching us having fun.

When you see the high cliffs what do you see?
I see cliffs up high in the sky doing nothing just standing proud.

Being at the seaside is so much fun for everyone
Having ice cream and playing in the sun.

Malicia Charles (11)
The Ridgeway Primary School, Reading

Water Fun

Water is blue,
It is used in a loo.

Puddles and sea,
Drinking tea,
Pools and wells,
Bucket and shells,
Water slides,
Ducking and dives,
Sprinkles splashing
People dashing.

Water is a pain,
When it's used in rain,
In the winter, autumn, spring,
Most of the time is rain, rain, rain.
In the summer is splash,
Splash, splash, fun, fun, fun,
Will you see the difference if I give you a water gun?

Sean Patten (11)
The Ridgeway Primary School, Reading

What Is Friendship?

What is friendship?
Is it a game or
Is it to worship?
Is it good or is it bad
Or can I find it out
From my best friend Pad?
Is it something I can
Remember or do I
Need some good advice?

Friendship is not a game,
It should be remembered
Friendship is my best friend,
I think it's yours too.

Alexandra Cotterell (10)
The Ridgeway Primary School. Reading

The King Of Quizzical Island

(Based on 'The King of Quizzical Island' by Gordon Snell)

The King of Quizzical Island
Had a most inquisitive mind.
He said, 'If I sail to the edge of the world
I wonder what I'll find?'

So he sailed up the muddy river
And he found himself in a vertical land,
There was a spotty, angry cloud
And he found lots of sand.

He said to himself, 'Where is the Ice Cream Mountain?'
When he saw the Ice Cream Mountain.
He jumped for joy, he jumped in and out of the fountain
And he saw a funny boy.

He saw chickens eat cakes and he joined in with them
He saw a strawberry jellyfish
And he picked up the jellyfish
And ate it on a dish.

He sailed back to another island
And when he turned back
He saw the land all back to normal
And after a minute they turned into sand.

Shatha Al-Siyabi (9)
The Ridgeway Primary School, Reading

The King Of Quizzical Island

(Based on 'The King of Quizzical Island' by Gordon Snell)

The King of Quizzical Island
Had an inquisitive mind.
He said, 'If I sail to the edge of the river
I wonder what I'll find?'

So he sailed over the dirty water
And saw an egg that was rough.
He saw dogs riding cycles
They were beating dogs they weren't very tough.

He found himself in a bubbly tree
And he saw dinosaurs playing snap
And saw thousands of marching fish
He saw three jumping jellyfish and they clapped.

He said, 'This is very, very fun'
He saw a golden mountain.
So he climbed to the top
And saw a very big fountain.

And sharks were eating clouds
Then he bumped on a falling star.
Then he ran away and fell into his boat
And then it turned into a big blue car.

Ebrina Drammeh (9)
The Ridgeway Primary School, Reading

The King Of Quizzical Island

(Based on 'The King of Quizzical Island' by Gordon Snell)

The King of Quizzical Island
Had a most inquisitive mind.
He said, 'If I sail to the edge of the world
I wonder what I'll find?'

So he sailed on the bright pink sea
With strawberries floating around.
There were bright orange dolphins
And then he found a pound.

Then he came to Mixy Wixy Island
He saw flying pigs in the air
And bananas having scones and tea
Then he saw a talking bear.

Next he went to see the bananas
And he enjoyed some scones and tea.
He met two blobs called Bob and Jim
Then he found a buzzy bee.

He went back home in a flying submarine
He found three chocolate ears.
He saw a multicoloured sky
And the yellow octopus cheers.

Hannah Hodge (9)
The Ridgeway Primary School, Reading

The King Of Quizzical Island

(Based on 'The King of Quizzical Island' by Gordon Snell)

The King of Quizzical Island
Had a most inquisitive mind.
He said, 'If I sail to the edge of the world
I wonder what I'll find?'

So he sailed on a flying boat and saw an angry sun,
He ate a strawberry jellyfish .
Then he played noughts and crosses with his feet
And made paper glasses on a dish.

Then he saw a cow flying in the air
Crabs dancing on the sand.
Then people eating grass
And chickens playing in a band.

The King on the way back sang a song called Strange Island
Which goes like this
'I've been to Strange Island
I had a great time.'

When he was finished he tried to escape
From the gigantic crocodile
And sailed faster and faster
Then fell down the Nile.

Louise Williams (9)
The Ridgeway Primary School, Reading

The King Of Quizzical Island

(Based on 'The King of Quizzical Island' by Gordon Snell)

The King of Quizzical Island
Had a most inquisitive mind.
He said, 'If I sail to the edge of the world
I wonder what I'll find?'

The sun made out of marshmallow
And talking liquorice trees
Munching on gorgeous ice cream
Nice curry and mushy peas.

There were red and gold chocolate bars
Monkey was eating a banana skin boat.
Looking at the red and gold sky
The octopus was wearing a red coat.

The fish were dancing in the sea
The dinosaurs drinking coffee.
He swam with a shark
Then sat down and ate a toffee.

Rebecca Bell (9)
The Ridgeway Primary School, Reading

The Sea

The sea is often roaring
It's very gentle too
It sounds so peaceful
With calm waves lapping.

The seagulls are swaying
Side to side
With their feathery soft wings
They love to collect different things.

The rocks are smoothed
By the sea's heavy waves
You can hear the splashing sound
Coming to the relaxing shore.

Lucy Dutton (10)
The Ridgeway Primary School, Reading

The King Of Quizzical Island

(Based on 'The King of Quizzical Island' by Gordon Snell)

The King of Quizzical Island
Had a most inquisitive mind.
He said, 'If I sail to the edge of the world
I wonder what I'll find?'

So he sailed on a chocolate boat
To find a stripy marshmallow jellyfish.
He saw dogs dancing round trees
And a flamingo making up a wish.

He found himself in an incredible land
Where pigs eat toffee and banoffee.
So the pigs sat down quietly
And had a cup of coffee.

The King stayed over at the flamingo house
And sat down and had a bun that was nice.
Could ever you see such a thing in your life
And three blind juicy mice.

Shannon Bailey (9)
The Ridgeway Primary School, Reading

Fairies

Fairies flutter through the sky.
They flutter, flutter by and by.
I hope, I hope they don't die.
They flutter, flutter through the sky.

Fairies flutter their magic dust.
I must, must not bust.
If it does you must die.
Because you can't fly.

She must look her best.
If she wants to be a princess.
Because the prince is wise and
He hates ties.

Charlotte King (10)
The Ridgeway Primary School, Reading

The King Of Quizzical Island

(Based on 'The King of Quizzical Island' by Gordon Snell)

The King of Quizzical Island
Had a most inquisitive mind.
He said, 'If I sail to the edge of the world
I wonder what I'll find?'

The sea was made of creamy caramel
He saw rabbits swimming with chocolate that wobbled.
The cows were skipping underwater
And the King gobbled up a cake and I mean gobbled.

The trees were made out of liquorice
There was Galaxy grass.
There was a Ripple lion coming near him
At night he laughed and laughed.

The King lay down under a liquorice tree, munching Galaxy grass
A blue cat went up to him and said, 'Hello'
A pile of leaves were munching fleas.

When he went on the wooden boat
He found a bottle
And he found some floats.

Lisa Dutton (9)
The Ridgeway Primary School, Reading

The King Of Quizzical Island

(Based on 'The King of Quizzical Island' by Gordon Snell)

The King of Quizzical Island
Had a most inquisitive mind.
He said, 'If I sail to the edge of the world
I wonder what I'll find?'

The sea was made of chocolate
And the fish were made of wine.
So he sat down peacefully
But he made an awful rhyme.

He rowed in this flowerpot
On the caramel lake.
He swam in a chocolate pond
Then munched on a Flake.

He was going home when his boat sank
And everything turned back to normal.

When the King got back,
He sang to his wife
Then they both went on holiday to Cornwall.

Kayley Emmett (9)
The Ridgeway Primary School, Reading

The King Of Quizzical Island

(Based on 'The King of Quizzical Island' by Gordon Snell)

The King of Quizzical Island
Had a most inquisitive mind.
He said, 'If I sail to the edge of the world
I wonder what I'll find?'

Dogs playing noughts and crosses,
Listening to rock music.
Monkeys playing simple tunes
A man putting his socks on.

Riding motorbikes with the chickens
Playing noughts and crosses with the dogs.
Dancing with the dogs
And riding a boat made out of logs.

On the way back everything changed back to normal.
He said, 'I don't want to go back there.
It's full of weird stuff,
Now it's time to stroke the cat.'

Jordan Alder (9)
The Ridgeway Primary School, Reading

The King Of Quizzical Island

(Based on 'The King of Quizzical Island' by Gordon Snell)

The King of Quizzical Island
He had a most inquisitive mind.
He said, 'If I sail to the edge of the world
I wonder what I'll find?'

The sun made out of marshmallow
And talking liquorice trees.
Munching on gorgeous ice cream and
Nice curry peas.

There was a red and gold chocolate bar,
The monkeys were eating banana skin boats.
Looking at the red and gold sky
The octopus was wearing a red coat.

The fish were dancing in the sea,
The dinosaurs were drinking coffee.
He swam with a shark,
He sat down and ate a wonderful toffee.

Yasmin Ali (8)
The Ridgeway Primary School, Reading

The King Of Quizzical Island

(Based on 'The King of Quizzical Island' by Gordon Snell)

The King of Quizzical Island
Had a most inquisitive mind.
He said, 'If I sail to the edge of the world
I wonder what I'll find?'

So he sailed up the river
He saw M&M fish.
He saw birds floating
And then he made a wish.

He saw a pencil walking a bottle
He saw a T-rex small and kind.
Chicks eating their mothers
What was he trying to find?

He had a chocolate party with the shops
He danced with the dogs in the streets
And with everyone also
That he'd met.

In the river he saw
Cats crunching their mothers
And crocodiles snapping
To the others.

Chelsea Cowley (9)
The Ridgeway Primary School, Reading

Lick Land

(Based on 'The King of Quizzical Island' by Gordon Snell)

The King of Quizzical Island
Had a most inquisitive mind.
He said, 'If I sail to the edge of the world
I wonder what I'll find?'

So he sailed through the lemonade sea,
And ate a chocolate shell.
He saw a bright blue jellyfish,
Who said, 'You really do smell!'

He found himself on Lick Land,
Where the rain's made of chocolate drops.
And jelly baby people and cats,
And talking trees wearing tops.

He stopped for tea with the jelly babies,
And borrowed a jumper from the trees.
He munched on marzipan flowers,
And stole honey from the bees.

Sailing back through the lemonade sea,
He saw a little whale.
The whale was unusual,
It had a bright red tail!

Toni Kelsey (9)
The Ridgeway Primary School, Reading

The King Of Quizzical Island

(Based on 'The King of Quizzical Island' by Gordon Snell)

The King of Quizzical Island
Had a most inquisitive mind.
He said, 'If I sail to the edge of the world
I wonder what I'll find?'

Chickens riding motorbikes
And a road made of skin.
Chickens riding skateboards
That are very thin.

He saw Coco Pops of stones
He ate bread but it was made out of bricks.
Then all the teeth fell out.

He looked back, it was normal
And far back he said,
'That was fun, now it's time for bed.'

Martin Hunt (9)
The Ridgeway Primary School, Reading

Crocodile

A crocodile has a strong fierce jaw,
One day it bit off someone's leg and broke the law.
A crocodile has got scaly skin,
When it was younger it used to play a violin.
This is a snappy one,
If you come near it, it will eat your thumb!

Omar Beaumont (10)
The Ridgeway Primary School, Reading

Two Little Kittens

Two little kittens,
One stormy night,
Began to quarrel,
And then to fight.

One little kitten said,
'That's my rat'
The other little kitten said,
'We'll see about that.'

They fought and they ran
To the hairy rat
Until the first little kitten
Fell over a mat.

They smashed the plates
And the glasses too.
Then one kitten did something bad
He had a great big poo.

They couldn't catch this sneaky rat
He was far too clever
Until they heard the door open
It was Grandad Trevor.

He jumped in the air in shock and worry
And the kittens saw from their sight
That the hungry dog
Might chase and bite.

The kittens were upset and sad
And promised that every night
They would not
Quarrel or fight.

Andrew Mwaki (10)
The Ridgeway Primary School, Reading

The King Of Quizzical Island

(Based on 'The King of Quizzical Island' by Gordon Snell)

The King of Quizzical Island
Had a most inquisitive mind
He said, 'If I sail to the edge of the world
I wonder what I'll find?'

So he sailed up the green, minty sea
To find two headed, chocolate fish
He saw pink, candyfloss clouds,
And had a marvellous dish.

He found himself in Opposite Island
Where the people barked and animals talked
All the giraffes were short
And trees started to walk.

Next he slid down the rainbow
And landed in a pot of gold
He saw pigs flying around
And saw them eating mould.

Sailing back to his Quizzical Island
And back to his sweet little bed
Off he slept in his lovely bed
And woke up to buy some bread.

Jinny Chonde (9)
The Ridgeway Primary School, Reading

The King Of Quizzical Island

(Based on 'The King Of Quizzical Island' by Gordon Snell)

The King of Quizzical Island
Had a most inquisitive mind
He said, 'If I sail to the edge of the world
I wonder what I'll find?'

So he sailed on a sparkly flying boat,
Through a rain coloured sky lightning
To talking eyeball clouds
Watching apple pies float by.

He saw a boat made of Mars bars.
A gold barking dog.
Some chocolate flying fish,
A pink dancing frog.

He danced with dinosaurs
He swam with a shark.
He ate table and chairs
And watched pussy cats park.

On the journey back to Quizzical Island.
He thought about all he had seen,
Such fun he'd had many friends he'd made.
Or was it just a dream?

David Annetts (9)
The Ridgeway Primary School, Reading

The King Of Quizzical Island

(Based on 'The King of Quizzical Island' by Gordon Snell)

The King of Quizzical Island
Had a most inquisitive mind.
He said, 'If I sail to the edge of the world
I wonder what I'll find?'

Sticky sweet chocolate houses,
All with chocolate gates.
Marshmallow families
Eating off wooden plates.

The King met Iceman
And Iceman taught the King some of his tricks.
And finally Iceman put a remote control together
And the King turned into sticks.

The King's boat had fallen down
So he sat down for a while to think.
He had an idea
And made the boat bright pink!

Karina Beckford (8)
The Ridgeway Primary School, Reading

The King Of Quizzical Island

(Based on 'The King of Quizzical Island' by Gordon Snell)

The King of Quizzical Island
Had a most inquisitive mind.
He said, 'If I sail to the edge of the world
I wonder what I'll find?'

So he sailed up the Green Grass River
On his chocolate brown boat.
The summer snow began to fall
And he put on his bright yellow coat.

He found himself on Incredible Island
Where dinosaurs were drinking coffee.
So he sat down very quietly
And ate one whole toffee.

It was a slimy ride back on the Green Grass River
So he called his lime cleaner Jack
As he waited for Jack
He had beans and liver.

Jonathan Ivell & Courtney Saunders (9)
The Ridgeway Primary School, Reading

Homework

In the middle of the night
I had a very big fright
'Cause I had some homework
And I thought it wasn't right.

I fell asleep that night
And I dreamt about the doubt
I thought I wouldn't shout
But I think the stupidest person
In my class could have got it right.

I wiggled here and there
I thought I wouldn't even dare
But I think I'll shave myself
Until I am completely bare.

I woke up this morning
I got dressed as quickly as my sister Darling
I went to school all the way strolling
When I gave my homework to my teacher
My heart was so much booming
At the end of the day
My teacher asked me to come this way
She said my homework was so right and the best she'd ever seen
I knew that!

Rachel Chonde (11)
The Ridgeway Primary School, Reading

The King Of Quizzical Island

(Based on 'The King of Quizzical Island' by Gordon Snell)

The King of Quizzical Island
Had a most inquisitive mind.
He said, 'If I sail to the edge of the world
I wonder what I'll find?'

So he sailed up the Co-Co Sea
To see thousands of mint stones,
And an eighteen-legged octopus
With dozens and dozens of bones.

When he got to Sweaty Island
He saw some sherbet sand.
He could also see jelly baby pirates
With lots of extra hands.

So he decided to eat the sand,
Fell asleep and went to bed.
He fell out the bed
And broke his head.

He went across the Co-Co Sea
Eating and eating everything as he went along.
He got fatter and fatter
Singing the magic song.

Georgia Cannon (9)
The Ridgeway Primary School, Reading

In The Garden

In the garden
Where the flowers
Are under the snow.

In the garden
Where you can kick the ball
Against a brightly coloured wall.

In the garden
Where we splash
In the puddles
With a mighty clash.

In the garden
When it starts to get cold
We write some words
Big and bold.

Terri Trimby (11)
The Ridgeway Primary School, Reading

A Friendship

A friendship is a lovely bond,
That goes on and on,
It is really fun,
When me and my friends play in the sun.

It is fun,
When my friends and I have chocolate fudge,
When we go to school,
We play the fool.

In the summer we play in my swimming pool,
And play pool,
We wash our hair,
And play fair,
This doesn't make sense,
But I don't care!

Vanessa Asongo (11)
The Ridgeway Primary School, Reading

Colourful Rabbits

There once was a young rabbit called Fink,
Whose fur was all fluffy and pink.
But one day it was hot
The rabbit was not
And the rabbit was no longer pink.

There once was an old rabbit called Due,
Whose fur was all fluffy and blue.
One day in his hutch
He had eaten too much
And blew up just like a balloon.

There once was a small rabbit called Ooun,
Whose fur was all fluffy and brown.
When he had first met a girl
He gave her a twirl
And got married in a brown dressing gown.

Joseph Brawn (11)
The Ridgeway Primary School, Reading

This Little Bear

This little bear didn't care
This little bear wasn't fair
This little bear was never there
Oh life, oh life wasn't fair
And nobody cared.

This little bear always cared
This little bear was more clever than ever
This little bear was the one I love forever.

This little bear was everybody's mate
This little bear was later than ever
This little bear was never clever
This little bear everybody hates
And was never your mate but he loved Kate.

Lannetha Williams (11)
The Ridgeway Primary School, Reading

The Rhyming Names

There was a young man called Joe,
He had a hairy toe,
When he grew older,
His toe was big as a boulder.

There was a man called Sam,
He liked eating ham,
His favourite animal was a lamb,
And he died of eating spam.

There was a man called Pat,
His favourite animal was a cat,
Who always lived on his mat,
And always ate five rats.

There was a lady in Peru,
Who lived in a big, fat shoe,
She went to sleep,
And had a fright,
And found out her dream was true.

Richie Locke (11)
The Ridgeway Primary School, Reading

The Old Man

There was an old man that lived in the shoe
There was a chicken that went *cock-a-do-a-do*
When the old man got into bed
He realised he had lost his head.

There was an old man that went to the shop
He had a dare that he could hop
When he got back, he dropped on the spot.

There was an old man that lay on the floor
He heard a knock on the door
So he decided to snore and leave the door
But he never got off the floor.

Tony Trimby (11)
The Ridgeway Primary School, Reading

We All Join In . . .

When we are eating our dinner with a crunch and a munch,
We all join in.
When we're waiting for a bath and our little brothers are splashing,
We all join in
When me and my friend wanted to go swimming and we both
                                                kept on jumping,
Then everyone joined in
When our dads are washing our pets,
We all want to join in.
When we're at school and we're waiting for the bell to go and our
                        friend was learning to count in nines
We all joined in.
When we're at home and we're waiting for something to do and
                        our mum is cleaning the dishes and cups,
We all feel like we want to join in.
When our mums are tidying our bedrooms,
We don't join in.
When our big sister is washing our clothes,
We don't join in.
When our dads want help with the painting,
We don't join in.
When our friend wants to play a game,
We all join in!

Tiah-Louise Flynn (10)
The Ridgeway Primary School, Reading

An Evacuee Poem

If I was an evacuee, I would scream and vibrate around the world.
If I was an evacuee, I would be mad as an elephant.
If I was an evacuee, I would run away as fast as a cheetah.
If I was an evacuee, my feelings would explode like a bomb.

Lucie Ellison (8)
Woodmansterne Primary School, Banstead

Similes And Metaphors

If I was the snow,
I would prance and dance around all day long until nightfall.
I would see all my white friends gathered around me.
I would be a beautiful looking snow lady
Identical to all the others like twins.
I would make everyone happy.
I would be free and wild.
If I was the sunset,
I would blow thousands of lovely hearts
And rose-red kisses to the world.
And make a wonderful love vortex
Of lots of sorts of pinks and yellows.

Claire Palmer (9)
Woodmansterne Primary School, Banstead

Similes And Metaphors

If I was the wind, I would punch the wall.
If I was the sun, I would erupt.
If I was a cloud, I would burst with rain.
If I was the wind, I would bark like a dog.
If I was the wind, I would run like a cheetah.

Harry Teal (9)
Woodmansterne Primary School, Banstead

Poem

If I was a soldier,
I would hear the whistling of a bullet and see the destruction
of a bomb.

If I was a soldier,
I would smell the smoke from the guns.

If I was a soldier,
I would fight as strong as a lion.

If I was a soldier,
I would be as scared as a mouse.

If I was a soldier,
My heart would be as cold as ice.

Caolan Quinn (9)
Woodmansterne Primary School, Banstead

Non-Fiction Poem

If I was the wind, I would blow like a fast train.
If I was the wind, I would sound like a screeching whistle.
If I was the rain, I would cry like a waterfall.
If I was the sun, I would be as bright as an erupting volcano.
If I was the wind, I would be invisible like a ghost.

Joseph Emanuel (8)
Woodmansterne Primary School, Banstead

Unicorns

A bright purple flash
Sparkled in the midnight air
In a quick second
A unicorn appeared
In a field by the mountains
The unicorn's mane shimmering
In the dark, dusky sky
His silky coat like spun gold.

Its sleek tail shimmering in darkness
Its shiny hooves clatter
Taking a big leap
Flying in a quick second
Its snowy white coat so beautiful.

When you pick a moon flower
Say the magic words
A pony transforms into a beautiful unicorn
Its snowy mane and a long wavy tail.

Charlotte Stokoe (9)
Woodmansterne Primary School, Banstead

Cats

The cat swiftly galloped across a soft, green blanket.
She raced up a tall tree to get her meal.
She feasted her eyes on her food.
She caught her dinner in a swift jump,
Ripped it apart meanly.
As the fiery sunset disappeared, she ran down the tall tree,
Off to look for her next delicious victim.

Brooke Jones (9)
Woodmansterne Primary School, Banstead

Collie Dog

Tail swishes like a skipping rope
Eyes sparkle like sapphires
Coat as gleaming as stars
As cuddly as a teddy bear.

As friendly as can be
Plays ball all day like a child
As playful as ever
Bursts like a balloon with joy.

Lauren Jennings (9)
Woodmansterne Primary School, Banstead

White Bengal Tiger

Her stripes are like a newspaper.
Her heart is as cold as ice.
She's as fierce as a devil.
Eyes are as sparkly as the moon.
Tail swishes like a whip.
Mouth drips with blood.
Kills like a gun.
Hunts like a hunter.

Megan Grover (9)
Woodmansterne Primary School, Banstead

The Snake

It slithers through the grass,
Eyes green, its body camouflaged
Just like an army officer.
Smells food,
Eyes trapped on its victim.

Joshua Noon (8)
Woodmansterne Primary School, Banstead

My Dog

My dog is lovely
His fur is pitch-black
When you talk to him
He barks back.

He is adorable
More than any dog
He's soppy, he's good
I love him a lot.

His eyes are as
Fantastic as anyone's
He's the cleverest dog
He's the best in the world.

Harry Cartwright (8)
Woodmansterne Primary School, Banstead

A Snake Poem

The alarming colour of the snake was blood-red and green as leaves.
Slithering through the hollow trees.
It smells like a horrid enemy,
It was hissing at me as if I was his next victim.
He took one bite and I felt the poison from his mouth.

Thomas McFarlane (9)
Woodmansterne Primary School, Banstead

Badgers

The badger's fur shone in the light of the harvest moon.
His beady, black eyes spied out his next meal.
He waddled after a slimy, fat, juicy slug and swallowed it whole!

Liam Turner (8)
Woodmansterne Primary School, Banstead

War

War is like no other place
It's where soldiers fight for lives,
Family and their country.

I look around, people injured and dead bodies lying still,
Blood swirls all around me as if I'm in a river,
People fall so quickly and suddenly.

I hear a bomb falling and exploding as it comes crashing down
Destroying everything that gets in its way.

I hear people screaming and crying
And guns shooting in every direction,
Soon the war has to end.

Georgia Thomas (10)
Woodmansterne Primary School, Banstead

White Tiger

As the white tiger drank from the freezing waterfall,
He spotted his dinner in the moonlight.
So he gracefully pounced across to his victim and ate him meanly.

Helena Paice (9)
Woodmansterne Primary School, Banstead

A Soldier's Life

If I was a soldier, my heart would cry.
If I was a soldier, my brain would die.
If I was a soldier, I would see the blood-drenched sun
                              a carpet of dead men.

Liam Andrews (9)
Woodmansterne Primary School, Banstead

The Fox

The fox was like a big ball of fire looking for a meal.
His horrid smell wafting behind him,
As he gleams around looking for meat.
No one dares to cross his path as he will just tear them apart.
Finally he finds a meal, he pounces at the animal.
The animal just stops and stares. No!
The animal is dead.

Marc Whittle (9)
Woodmansterne Primary School, Banstead

Panthers

Emerald eyes which seek out my opponents.
A runner of power.
My midnight body camouflaged by the night sky.
My paws turn into viper claws.
My victim has seen me and it freezes in horror.
I've killed, I've won!
I'm a killer!
I'm a panther!

Sam McFarland (10)
Woodmansterne Primary School, Banstead

Leopard

The fiery coat burning through the forest.
The leopard sees an animal.
He goes running through the trees.
The animal is cornered.
He pounces and has his lunch.

Tom Murray (8)
Woodmansterne Primary School, Banstead